TH_ _____ OF
BURBAGE WHARF

STEAM THRESHING AND
PLOUGHING CONTRACTORS
OF WILTSHIRE

A FAMILY HISTORY

BY

JOHN NEWTON

© Copyright 1995 John Newton

ISBN 0-9508480-3-4

Published by The Road Locomotive Society
Printed by Amadeus Press Ltd, Huddersfield
Typesetting by Highlight Type Bureau Ltd, Bradford

THE FALL STORY

ACKNOWLEDGEMENTS

THE EARL OF CARDIGAN
MRS DOLLY DEACON
MISS MOLLY FALL
MRS HILDA FALL AND THE LATE MR HARRY FALL
MR JOHN ALLEN
THE LATE MR J BOUGHTON
C J BROWN
DR JONATHON BROWN - ARCHIVIST - THE RURAL HISTORY CENTRE,
UNIVERSITY OF READING
MRS BETTY CHANTER
MR S J COOPER
MR W DENNIS
THE LATE ALAN DUKE - FORMER RECORDS OFFICER
ROAD LOCOMOTIVE SOCIETY
MR (CURLEY) FREWIN
MR D J FULKER - ARCHIVIST KENNET & AVON CANAL TRUST
MR LEN GRIFFITHS
MR R A HARDING - RECORDS OFFICER ROAD LOCOMOTIVE SOCIETY
MR DOUGLAS SMITH

I ALSO ACKNOWLEDGE WITH SINCERE GRATITUDE THE HELP RECEIVED FROM MY WIFE BRENDA DURING THE COMPILATION OF THIS WORK, TOGETHER WITH MS JANET AMISON WHO PAINSTAKINGLY TYPED MY MANUSCRIPT AND THOSE WHO HAVE HELPED WITH PHOTOGRAPHS. TO ANY OTHERS WHOM I MAY HAVE INADVERTENTLY OMITTED, I CRAVE FORGIVENESS FOR MY OVERSIGHT, BUT NEVERTHELESS ACKNOWLEDGE.

FOREWORD

It was both a surprise and a pleasure to be asked to contribute the Foreword for this, John Newton's second book. The story of the Falls of Burbage Wharf is one that was mirrored many times over throughout the land but it is none-the-less interesting for that. The history of English agriculture and the way in which it evolved is an important one; the particular interest of farm mechanisation and the use of steam power is but a small segment within that history. However, it is the use of the steam road vehicle in all its forms that is the particular concern of the Road Locomotive Society and also one of the reasons for John's interest in the family central to this narrative. The publication of this book by the Society is something of a new departure, for while the Society has been responsible for publishing a number of technical books, albums of photographs and reprints of manufacturers' catalogues, it has not previously published a work of social history.

Agricultural contracting became common place from the time when steam driven machinery for thrashing and cultivation was introduced. The simple reason was that the engines and tackle were too expensive for the average farmer to own and in any case would have been too little used. It therefore made sense for specialists to own the equipment and for them to provide a service to the farming community. The area covered by a contractor was generally quite small and consisted of a regular round, particularly for thrashing. Steam ploughing was also practised on a regular basis although it was not always an annual event because of the patterns of cropping which were traditionally followed. It should be understood that steam ploughing was carried out using two large traction engines, one either side of the field, hauling by cables the plough or other implement backwards and forwards between them. As the work progressed, the engines moved the width of the tilled strip along the headlands after each pass of the implement. When ploughing, as many as seven furrows could be tilled at each pass and when cultivating, up to fifteen tines could be pulled creating a strip of tillage up to eight feet wide.

In this book, John has chronicled the rise and decline of a family business that provided a service to a relatively small area as both ploughing and thrashing contractors. That the family concern involved being wharfingers, coal merchants, milk producers and retailers as well as contractors creates an interesting overall picture and certainly sets this story apart from many others. Interwoven with the main theme of the Fall family are many other facets of life within Savernake Forest and the Vale of Pewsey which will make this work appeal to those whose interest is other than in steam engines. The history of these small businesses is very important and well worth the time and effort involved in recording. Sadly much information has now been lost and what we have is that much more valuable. I applaud John for his enterprise in producing this work and commend it to all who have an interest in traction engines or in the local history of the area.

John has had a lifetime interest in traction engines, his forebears having been thrashing and ploughing contractors in the Romney Marsh area of Kent as told in his previous book "Steam In My Family". Though not an engineer, John is a true enthusiast and preservationist being an engine owner and long standing Chairman of the Thames Valley Traction Engine Club. He has also taken a keen interest in the Civic affairs of his home town of Hungerford where he has held the office of Constable for periods of three and two years. As a result of this service he has become a Freeman of The City of London.

Peter Smart
June 1995

Some surviving nameplates from the Fall family engines.

INTRODUCTION

As a small boy, I well recall sitting in our farmhouse kitchen where, over a cup of tea, my late father talked with a Mr Fall. His regular visits concerned the quantity of milk being produced by the estate over which my father was manager. Following my late mother's bidding of "Say good afternoon to Mr Fall", I became intrigued by the conversation which, having quickly dispensed with the business in hand, soon turned to the topic of steam ploughing. As the time passed, their conversation became more animated and I listened intently to the stories they had to tell.

Who was this man with whom my father had so much in common? They talked the same language - it being not forgotten that, in my father's case, only a few years had then elapsed since he reclaimed much of this estate using steam ploughing engines [about which facet of his life I have already written in "STEAM IN MY FAMILY" - Published by Meresborough Books in 1988]. Whilst in Mr Fall's case I soon learnt that he was one of a local steam contracting family of high repute, who had himself only ceased working with steam engines a few years previously. Little wonder then that these two gentlemen had much to reminisce about, even though they were ignorant at the time that, within a decade or so, the steam preservation movement would come into being.

Many years were to elapse after those afternoon meetings before I, in due time, joined the preservation scene. Imagine my delight therefore to find in doing so that 'Mr Fall' and his younger brother Bill were thus involved. During the following decade or so I got to know them particularly well and I also was able to learn a little of their family's history - and the role they had played in the sphere of steam threshing and ploughing contracting, in their native Wiltshire.

Subsequent to this, I revelled in Bill's company at many engine events, which he attended on one of two steam rollers, that had been purchased and restored by his friend Cecil Brown, then a dairy farmer on the outskirts of Newbury. Firstly an 8 ton single cylinder Aveling and Porter Roller No. 10762 of 1923 Registration MF4008, and latterly another Aveling and Porter - a 10 ton machine No. 10997 of 1924 Registration MO3687 which they named 'The Enborne Queen'. This latter engine had been mechanically restored by the firm of James and Crockerell of Durrington, Wiltshire and beautifully painted and lined out by travelling showman of great renown James Williams of Tadley. What times we had in one another's company - Bill was always ready for a laugh and ready for a pint! Similarly, elder brother Harry undertook the local round of rallies for a few years also on a duo of steam rollers that he owned at that time. Firstly a diminutive 6 ton Aveling and Porter No. 11618 of 1926 known as "Poppet" which he had purchased from the firm of W Marshall Ltd of Charlton near Andover, Hants who carried on the trade of builders and general contractors - and then one of the last steam engines to be manufactured anywhere in Great Britain, a 10 ton roller, by Marshall Sons & Co Ltd of Gainsborough, No. 89549 of 1944. To see these men driving steam engines, was to witness a man at one with himself - they both possessed a stance and "rightness" upon an engine that can only come about by years of experience and natural ability.

Sad to say I never met Jack, the eldest of the three 'boys' who rightfully commands much space in this narrative. However whilst undertaking research for this work, I have had the good fortune to meet, and get to know, the brothers' elder twin sisters and in so doing have gained a real understanding of their family life.

For my part I have tried as best I can to faithfully record this family's farming enterprise which spanned more than a century during a spectacular period of agricultural development - the era of the steam engine - a period of time during which many pages of our agrarian history were indeed being set down for posterity. It behoves us all to document it and listen to their tales - for they were there.

J. Newton
November 1994

AVELING & PORTER No. 10762 of 1923 MF4008 4 hp 8 ton, single cylinder, owned by C. J. BROWN. DRIVER: BILL FALL. c. late 1960's.

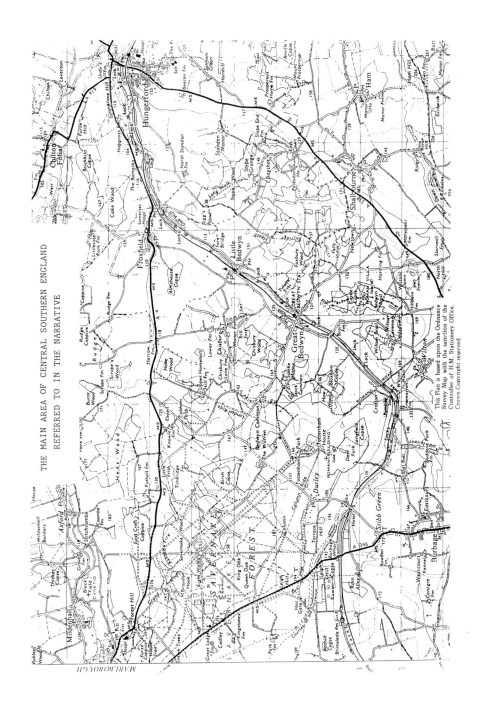

THE MAIN AREA OF CENTRAL SOUTHERN ENGLAND
REFERRED TO IN THE NARRATIVE

This Plan is based upon the Ordnance Survey Map with the sanction of the Controller of H.M. Stationery Office. Crown Copyright reserved.

CHAPTER I

Proof that from the earliest of time man has planted his footsteps and lived in the area of central southern England has been well documented. This is further enforced by the many ancient relics and scars that have been left upon the landscape which give credence to this statement. In the first instance significant amounts of flint artefacts have subsequently been unearthed which had been fashioned by primitive man, whose lifestyle was that of a hunter of no fixed abode. Followed in turn by perhaps the most striking relics, those of the standing stone circles of Stonehenge and Avebury that today number amongst the world's most famous monuments to an ancient civilisation; huge works, the toil of countless thousands of men who laboured in honour of their gods. Then came those who wished to commemorate their dead by building large earth mounds in which to inter the cremated remains of their chieftains, namely the long barrows, all eclipsed by the most striking earthwork of all - Silbury Hill. A growing population, with its attendant need for increased food production, which corresponded with a more stable style of living, brought about increasing conflict between neighbouring tribes, whose period of evolution is again clearly marked by the several hillforts contained within the region; places of refuge when threatened, in time of war.

The Wansdyke, an early excavation, also strides across this landscape - formed to create a boundary between the Belgic and aboriginal tribes of ancient Britain, as also does the historic trading route - Europe's oldest roadway - the Ridgeway bisect this area. Coming forward in time, the arrow-straight roads of the Roman conquest are clearly defined, as they criss-cross the land joining their principal cities - all constructed using the slave labour of those they had subjugated.

The aforementioned items are but few of the marks of succeeding generations left upon their vast area of our island home. Many others remain which are instantly recognisable when glimpsed, by even the most cursory glance at a modern ordnance survey map, all clearly defined by the familiar symbols of the cartographer's art. A larger scale version of which, will show, nearby the centre of the area, the site of one of the bloodiest battles to have been fought between the armies of the ancient kingdoms of Wessex and Mercia. This took place in the year 675AD, and is recorded as The Battle of Bedwyn.

Of more modern times, man's premier routes of communication are highlighted; principal amongst which are the main road - the A4 -joining the capital city of London to the famed regency spa city of Bath; together with the Kennet and Avon Canal, - a staggering earthwork of the industrial age, constructed to unite the tideways of the Thames and Bristol Channel - and the iron roadway of the former Great Western Railway. Midway between the aforementioned cities of London and Bath, and bordered on its northern boundary by the main road lies a large tract of woodland, roughly triangular in shape - coloured green on today's modern maps - over which the words Savernake Forest are printed. This area has as its boundary at its southernmost edge, both the canal and railway, at a point where they almost join, which lies just north of the ancient village of Burbage and is known as Burbage Wharf, which is central to my story, as it is at the farm of this name that the family about whom I write, lived, loved and worked for over one hundred years. More than a century in which they carried on their chosen trade of farming, dairying, steam threshing and ploughing contracting, as well as Wharfingers for the canal - a capacity in which they served from its era of most prosperity until its decline. Over a century of service to the local community during which time they carried not only the friendship, but the respect of their neighbours to such a degree that their name became synonymous with the village, which commands the entrance to the fertile Vale of Pewsey, and known to all over a wide area as "The Falls of Burbage Wharf".

However, before commencing my tale of the family, and its agrarian enterprise, it is necessary to elucidate a little upon how this family whose origins were in Yorkshire, came to be farming within the bounds of this forest area, and to tell a little of its unique fascinating history.

An engine boiler washout pump (c. 1870's).

10

CHAPTER II

Prior to the Norman Conquest, a tract of land which included the forest, lay in the possession of one by the name of Aluric - a Saxon who had held the land and the manor of Burbage, a small village settlement on the southern outskirts of the forest, since the time of Edward the Confessor.

Following the conquest by William, Duke of Normandy, Aluric became dispossessed of his home and his lands, by a Norman knight, by the name of Richard Esturmy, who held the forest on behalf of his Sovereign. An example by which the Duke not only rewarded those whose service had been valuable during his campaign, but of ensuring by placing large areas of his newly claimed territory under the auspices of his trusted friends and family members, he would better be able to control and subjugate its inhabitants. For his tenure, Richard paid only a nominal rent and was required to perform only two duties. These were to administer his lands and protect the forest to the satisfaction of his Monarch and to provide one soldier, fully armed and mounted, to serve at any time in the King's army "within the seas" - that is to say, against the Welsh and Scots. Thus it was that Richard Esturmy became the first Warden of Savernake Forest, and in so doing established a line that has continued down through successive generations until the present day. Over 900 years in which the Wardenship of the great forest area has been administered largely by only three families - the fortunes of which, like the forest itself, have waxed and waned in an alarming way, and which in so doing have mirrored the history of our nation. Whole pages of our island history have been written deep within the forest, which has been home to King and commoner alike and which holds its place unique within the Realm.

Under the system of Wardenship instigated by William, and carried out hereabouts by Richard, those who lived within its bounds, either in villages or hamlets or scattered deep within the forest, were subjected to Forest Law - a fierce law of order by which the King, through his Wardens, was able to keep check on his people and over which he could wield immense power. Thus it can be clearly seen, that by allowing the forest area of land to increase in size, the King's power could be similarly enhanced. This system had been allowed to advance to such a state, that by the time of accession to the throne by King John, not only were huge tracts of land under forest - including his own New Forest - but his rule of law smacked at 'absolutism' - this led to great discontent amongst the barons who forced upon him the Magna Carta, in the signing of which he promised to rule according to the laws and customs of the Realm and which also contained provision for radical disforestation. Interestingly, the only person to sign the Great Charter as a witness to the King's hand, beside the barons present, was the then Lord Mayor of London. In doing so this 'commoner' became the first person outside the nobility to play a part in the affairs of the nation, which, centuries later, was to be known as democracy.

Significant as the signing of this charter was during King John's Reign, another signed parchment by that same King had even more bearing upon Savernake Forest: the then warden, Henry Esturmy, great great grandson of Richard, was able to solicit a further charter from his Sovereign, which was sealed on 28th April 1200 at Porchester and conferred their hereditary title as Wardens of Savernake Forest. This was indeed a fortuitous step, for many times during the intervening centuries has the value of that precious document been sorely tested, as successive wardens either found favour or fell foul of the Monarch of the day. Whilst in other circumstances, when upon the death, either untimely or otherwise, of the natural successor to the title, the heir being a minor - an occasion when the line could more easily be usurped, it became necessary for the Constables of Marlborough to assume these responsibilities until such time as the rightful heir became of age. Bearing the great seal of England, and in the King's name, the succession of the title of warden from father to son was as a matter of right, the hereditary nature of this being beyond question. However, it was essential even then for the warden to keep the King's favour as the land under his control was attached to the 'office' of Warden and not to the 'holder' of the office!

This valuable document was not however the only prized possession in the hands of the wardens down through the ages. A magnificent silver-tipped ivory hunting horn pre-dating the charter of King John, has reputedly been held as a badge of office by the incumbent warden from the time of King Henry II. It is believed to have been presented by the King to the son of the forest's first warden, also Richard, to be used as a salute when he visited his royal 'demesne'. It was probably the customary greeting from the warden to the King when they met during the Monarch's visits for hunting.

Now doubly secure with the charter and the Esturmy horn, line of succession of hereditary warden has passed down from generation to generation to the present day. Twice during the intervening nine centuries it has passed via the female line. The first such instance being after more than three centuries of Esturmy wardenship, when, upon the death of Sir William in 1427, he having no male heir, it passed through his daughter to her son John Seymour. Then began an association with the forest by that family that was to witness, without doubt, the most momentous years and happenings that history accords this magnificent area of land. Indeed it was the fourth generation of Seymour wardens and the third by name of John, later Sir John, who found lasting favour with his Sovereign King Henry VIII, in that the King took the hand of his daughter Jane, as his third wife. History records that the occasion was one of much rejoicing, shared by many of the local nobility and tenantry and was conducted in the Great Barn of

Wolf Hall in the forest, the day after her predecessor Anne Boleyn was executed at the tower. This rejoicing however, was to be short lived, Jane dying in childbirth not eighteen months after her wedding.

Similarly, it was the unfortunate Jane's Uncle Edward, who was elevated to Duke of Somerset and later conferred Earl Marshal and Lord Treasurer who upon the succession, at the age of ten, of Edward VI (following the death of his father Henry VIII) attained such a powerful position within the realm, only to fall from grace accused of usurping the Royal Authority. He was imprisoned in the Tower and executed before his construction of a new mansion home planned for the forest had hardly been commenced. Nevertheless at the height of his power he was able to solicit letters patent from the young King Edward VI, so that the whole forest over which he was its fifteenth hereditary warden, passed to him and ceased to be 'Crown' property. This act set Savernake firmly apart from every other such area of land - it becoming the only private woodland area designated 'forest', a unique title which continues today, as all remaining such areas in a subject's hands are titled 'chase'.

Thus Savernake was safe again and remained in the hands of the Seymour family until, upon the death of John - the fourth Duke of Somerset in 1678, it passed again for the second time only via the female line of Lady Elizabeth Seymour to her husband of two years, Thomas Bruce, the eldest son of the Earl of Ailesbury. It is the family of Bruce , now more correctly named Brudenell-Bruce who today carry out the responsibilities of hereditary warden. Thus it is that the three aforementioned families have administered to the needs of this ancient woodland for over nine centuries.

In this brief mention of nearly one thousand years of our history, I have not recorded the happenings within the forest itself. Suffice it to say that as successive wardens took up their birthright, so too did they assume their responsibilities to a greater or lesser degree. There were those whose grasp of their history and heritage led them to live with all humility, devoting their energies almost exclusively to the wellbeing of their vast estate and the rehabilitation of their forest. Vast planting schemes were implemented which they themselves would never live to see in splendour, many to the designs of the greatest authorities of their day, including Capability Brown. Others virtually abandoned their landed estates as they chose to indulge in politics or war-mongering, whilst others sought to live the life of a nobleman to the full, entertaining their Monarch and his court in splendid style, to the detriment of their inheritance. Again, others saw fit to build for themselves magnificent houses, as befit their title, Tottenham House in the forest; whilst in the City - Somerset House.

Fortunately for Savernake's sake, there always appeared to be one waiting in the wings who would rise in due time to redress the deficiencies of those who preceded him. Undoubtedly the greatest of these, and the one who has been acknowledged as the 'Saviour of Savernake', was Henry, the fifth Marquess of Ailesbury, the twenty-seventh hereditary warden, who succeeded to the title in 1894. It was his nephew William who led a life of such excess and had by the age of twenty-one years, amassed debts of £170,000 - so reducing the fortunes of his family, that the sale of the estate seemed the only way of redressing the situation. To Lord Henry's great credit he chose an altogether different path. Incensed, by the thought of losing all that had been held for so long by his forebears in the office of warden - he resisted the temptation to sell, choosing instead to part with his vast estates in Yorkshire. These had come into the family by gift of the first Stuart King to Lord Bruce of Kinloss almost three centuries before - their sale was a grievous blow to the old Marquess, who visited those familiar places 'one last time' in 1886 - a broken and sad man. He now turned his remaining energies towards rebuilding his Wiltshire estate and embarked upon a massive tree planting scheme.

He succeeded to such a degree that his heir Chandos the sixth Marquess of Ailesbury when writing of the forest that he loved described it thus:-

"Those who remember the forest park - which aged, but changed little, until about 1940 - will however recall as perhaps its most striking and unusual feature the fact that it defied a familiar proverb. Ordinarily, on a woodland park or ride, it is true that "you can't see the wood for the trees". At Savernake this was not so; for the trees were well spaced and, being hardwoods, they had not grown at all in the many valleys or bottoms where the frost was wont to strike. Thus one continually came on open glades where nature had worked as the ally of art.

There was moreover no undergrowth, other than bracken - the deer having killed all the bushes or part-grown trees which, in an ordinary woodland, combine to limit one's ground level view to perhaps fifty yards. At Savernake, the visitor might disturb a fallow buck which had been lying in the bracken's shade, and he could then follow it with his eye as it plunged away into the distance. He would see it pause just beyond bow-shot, turning to eye him mistrustfully - and he could still follow it as it resumed its flight. Maybe it would cross a glade, where sudden sunlight would illuminate its dappled markings, re-entering woodland beyond. Only after some quarter of a mile would the intervening tree trunks at last close it off from his sight. It was very delightful thus to be amongst the trees".
Reproduced with due acknowledgement to its author.

CHAPTER III

It was in the mid-1850's when a young man left his native Yorkshire home and moved to Warren Farm, Savernake to take up his position as farm bailiff. His name was John Fall. I believe it not to be a coincidence that this young agriculturalist should make this considerable journey, leaving behind his family - many of whom, as his descendants, still reside in those northern shires. For it is well documented that in 1856 the first Marquess of Ailesbury died, his successor to his title being George Frederick Brudenell-Bruce.

The second Marquess not only took great pride in his inheritance, but conceived a plan to transform it, together with Tottenham Park in and around his magnificent mansion, into "one great whole". To achieve this he had taken down the fences which had formerly separated the Deer Park from the forest and other various enclosures which had been erected by his predecessors. He then undertook the erection of a completely new deer fence around the whole area which, upon completion, measured a total length of some sixteen miles. This enclosed land largely took on a park-like setting, and encompassed many of the finest trees, the legacy of previous wardens. The deer roamed free in this setting, which was recognised upon its completion in 1870 as being comparable only to that of the sovereign, namely Windsor Great Park!

However, it was in the first decades of the previous century, when Charles Bruce, the Earl of Ailesbury was in tenure, that Warren Farm received its first mention - then as "Home Farm". He kept it "well-stocked" and it comprised extensive farm buildings and stables which he enlarged by disforesting land which had previously formed a great part of Havering Heath. The second Marquess now again increased the size of this farm by the addition of a large area of land to the north and east sides of his magnificent mansion home Tottenham House which had become available during the creation of his Forest Park as described above.

Since the earliest of times, it would seem that varying numbers of commoners of the villages and hamlets lying within the perimeter of the large forest area, had had rights of pasture and pannage, whilst others claimed the right to graze horses. Those people had farmed on the old manorial system, where large fields were carved up into strips which were farmed on a communal basis. However, following the Enclosure Acts of the eighteenth century these strips gave way to the system whereby each man farmed his own enclosed area in the way he wished. It was the gradual joining together of their small uneconomic areas of land into larger units which brought about the larger farms of today.

However, by the arrival of John Fall at Warren Farm in the mid-1850's only this farm, the 'Home Farm' on the estate would appear to have been of any appreciable size - its requirement to provide the needs as befitting a nobleman of the day perhaps being its 'raison d'etre' - surprisingly therefore it is recorded, that this was a farm largely pasture in nature. The clue to this lies most probably in the name - Warren Farm. It is known and already related, that the large portion of the farm at that time had evolved from the clearing of heathland, whilst another significant area had been added from within the former smaller deer park. Obviously this land had been home to many thousands of rabbits which, since their introduction into these islands at the time of the Norman Conquest, had multiplied enormously. Nevertheless, in defence of this endearing animal I record, that do much damage though it may - man had introduced it into this land from the continent as a year round source of food. A role that it fulfilled admirably - becoming a major portion of the staple diet of many sections of the populace, especially the more lowly paid agricultural and industrial labourers, without which, their diet - never substantial, would oft-times have been meatless. This, long before man, in all his evil and hostility, introduced the horrific disease of myxomatosis. I digress; to return to my narrative - therefore given the above parameters of this farm, and with free rein to the deer within the park - it seems almost inevitable that grazing and not corn growing was predominant upon the acres of Warren Farm.

As previously stated also, I believe John Fall's arrival to have not been coincidental, as at this time his employer owned large estates in Yorkshire, to which he returned on a regular basis. It is not therefore beyond probability that those engaged upon those estates should learn of the existence of Savernake, and even desire to move south under the same patronage - especially if this move could increase their station in life. This is what happened I believe to John Fall. Whether or not his parents were in the employ of the second Marquess, as tenant farmers perhaps? I know not - but enjoy the confidence of his employer he certainly did, to such a degree that, I have been told, it was part of his duties when engaged at Warren Farm (the home farm) to ensure that the cellars of the nearby mansion were kept well stocked!

Presumably, settling to his duties well, this young man soon attracted the attention of the daughter of the nearby vicar of Great Bedwyn - the Reverend Ward. However the worthy cleric frowned upon this association, stating that a farmer was not good enough to take the hand of his beloved Elizabeth. This was eclipsed however by the young couple returning to John's home in Yorkshire, where he married his thirty-one year old bride retracing their steps to set up their own home at Warren Farm in June 1861.It was here that their family, eventually to number five were born. Firstly John in 1862, then William in 1864, Cissie in 1865 George Mason in 1866 and Annie in 1869.

That the family prospered whilst living at Warren Farm, is not in question, but with the need to further himself once again, and to provide increased security for their growing family, John Fall took a bold step - this was to become a farmer in his own right. It must be remembered, that whilst still under the employ of George Frederick the second Marquess - who undoubtedly was fond of him - John's role as bailiff of the home farm was secure. However, past history had shown that sometimes with the change of heritary warden, radical alterations in the way in which the forest and its vast estate were farmed had taken place. Whilst still under his familiar employer, it would seem advantageous to branch out on his own account which he did by securing the tenancy of Wharf Farm, Burbage in the year 1874.

Hilda Fall's painting of Burbage Wharf, c. 1850's.

CHAPTER IV

The choice of Wharf Farm as his home by John Fall, and its tenancy becoming vacant at a convenient time for him, was fortunate indeed. Even if it contained only 60 acres and lay within the southern-most tip of the then forest area, there were however three major items which would have made it attractive to him. Firstly the opportunity presented itself of farming on his own account, and in this connection the pasture land nearby the farmstead was supported by sufficient farm buildings to make dairying a mainstay of his new enterprise. Secondly, the Wharf Farm took its name from the nearby Kennet and Avon Canal, which flowed right alongside the farmyard - the wharf of which at this busy coming together of road, rail and water was included in his tenancy - he becoming the Wharfinger[1.] This second source of income, though well-earned in the effort required, was invaluable, especially as this section of the canal which was opened at the completion of 'The Cut' from Newbury to Bath in 1810, was now enjoying the halcyon days of its existence. Thirdly, in taking over the tenancy of Wharf Farm he took over (presumably at the outgoing sale of the previous tenant) a steam threshing contracting business. This latter statement I have as yet (as I write) been unable to substantiate - but have been led to believe is correct. Should this be the case, then undoubtedly this threshing contracting business - for that is what it must have been, as his own farm was insufficient in size to warrant either the outlay or use of such equipment - would have formed one of the earliest outfits to operate as such in the locality, following the near total loss of these earliest forms of mechanised threshing which had been smashed, during the period of the 'swing riots' in the first decades of that century.

Whilst all of the above would have appealed to the new tenant farmer, coupled with the threefold opportunity which they presented for making a living, I am quite sure that at the outset the considerable outlay necessitated by them would have brought about its own anxiety. Not so, I am sure, would have been the appeal to his wife Elizabeth. Even though the farmhouse at The Warren was a substantial, well-built dwelling within easy walking distance of both church and school at St Katherines, the farmhouse at the wharf was no less so. It stood beside the roadway, at the side of the entrance to the farmyard and wharf and comprised two principal reception rooms, a large farmhouse kitchen with a larder, back kitchen, dairy and pump room off, whilst upstairs three bedrooms of fine proportions were well arranged with two attic rooms suitable for maids above. This was a secure home in which to raise her growing family. The buildings which complemented the house (besides those of the farmstead) and which were connected with the portion of the tenant's business that related to the canal wharf, comprised a large brick and stone built granary, a weighbridge, and a substantial stable block with standing for sixteen horses. In addition to which a large wooden-beamed hand wound wharf crane stood at the water's edge and which today, recently restored, stands as a tangible reminder of that area's important role.

Even though the wharf at Burbage was a privately owned one - by the Marquis of Ailesbury's estate - nevertheless the role of the wharfinger was a busy one, many and varied being his duties. There were firstly the many barges that passed through in both directions carrying cargoes of great variety. These included coal (coming up from the docks) which had originated either in South Wales or the Somerset coalfields, to be dropped off en route or as a through cargo to Reading and beyond; and stone from Bath and the Mendip Hills for building and construction work. Whilst either as a return cargo or a load in its own right, a great tonnage of corn - predominantly wheat - headed towards the docks at Bristol, either for export or milling. As would be expected, given the nature of the area, there were many barges laden with timber and timber products on the canal. Not all of these were just passing through, however, as many timber cargoes either originated from or were off-loaded at Burbage Wharf. In almost every instance large horses would require some attention either for overnight accommodation or just a brief respite during loading or unloading times. Similarly, local merchants, estates and farmers would require the same service for their draught horses during their visits to the wharf, for which the wharfinger would make a charge.

Also essential to the remuneration of the wharfmaster was the role played by both the weighbridge and the wharf crane. Given that, in relationship to the former (the weighbridge) the weight of timber in the round could be calculated by the use of Hoppus's measurer, and in sawn form it could be measured by the cube, and grain totalled by the sack - the quarter in those days. The necessity for checking these calculations and the true weight of other commodities could only be accurately assessed by use of the weighbridge.

As regards the latter (the wharf crane), evidence exists in the form of several wharfage crane tickets which have survived from that period. These tickets bear credence to the almost constant use of that all-important piece of apparatus, whilst at the same time clearly illustrate the types of cargo being loaded and unloaded. The majority of tickets are unsigned, but an exciting exception is one signed by John Fall dated August 12th 1887. It concerns the loading of 77 sacks of wheat from a Mrs Gale onto a barge named 'Kennet' owned by James Dews under the captaincy of John Aldridge. The weight of grain loaded equalled 8^1/$_2$ tons, for which the cranage/loading charge was two shillings and a penny halfpenny, i.e. 2/11^1/$_2$d or 11p. Another unsigned ticket from the same period makes for interesting reading, in that it records on May 4th 1887 the barge owned by Robbins and

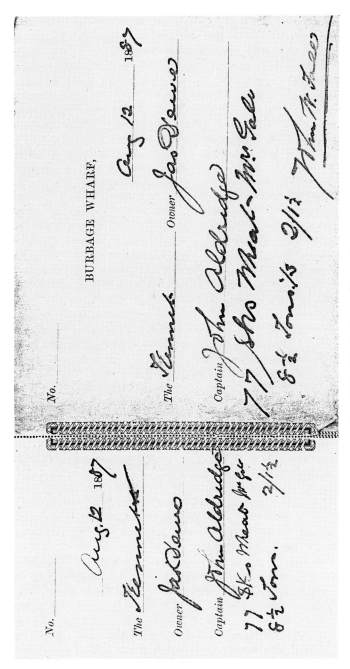

Wharf Ticket for the barge 'Kennet'

Co under Captain William Harding was loaded with 18 tons of timber, consigned to Honey Street to the premises of Messrs Robbins Lane and Pinnegar further down the canal - for which the loading charge was again 2/11½d (11p). Amongst other tickets we find mention that: "On March 18th 1897 the barge 'Unity' brought to the Wharf from Honey Street weatherboarding taken away by Lord Ailesbury: W.Harding - Captain". There is also evidence of hurdles and straw being carried as cargoes. Hurdles, which more than likely were made deep in the adjoining forest by local craftsmen, and straw which most probably was destined for Bath or Bristol, for use in city stables. A fee was also due to the wharfinger for assistance given when turning barges. Thus it can be clearly demonstrated and understood that, from the time of the commencement of his tenancy of this farm the working canal, even though then under the ownership of the Great Western Railway (since 1852) and kept open by them under an Act of Parliament - demanded a high level of close personal supervision and commitment from the wharfinger, but as aforesaid contributed a valued percentage of his income.

However, quite how this was made up I know not, because as the wharf was a private one owned by the Marquess and his estate, it therefore was not listed amongst those wharves that were agents and toll collectors for the Kennet and Avon Canal. I therefore presume that the wharfinger (John Fall) had an internal arrangement with his landlord - perhaps on a percentage basis or even as a reduced rent for his farm for services rendered by him at the wharf. What is certain, however, is that for a considerable period of years during his and his family's tenancy of the wharf, its operation contributed substantially to their livelihood. An illustration of the role played by the wharf at that time can be gleaned by reference to a painting which survives, the date of which is unknown and undoubtedly contains a certain amount of artistic licence. Nevertheless it portrays the hustle and bustle of a busy working yard - featuring both man, the horse and the barge. (See Page 17).

Having briefly mentioned Messrs Robbins Lane and Pinnegar Limited above, I deem it pertinent here to expound a little upon that firm, especially as its role in connection with Burbage Wharf and upon the Kennet and Avon Canal itself was of paramount importance to its trading viability at that time. Situated at Honey Street, a few miles west of the wharf, just beyond Pewsey, they advertised themselves in the local press as "English and Foreign Timber Merchants and Importers - Sawing and Planing Mills - Buyers of all classes of English Timber". What they do not go on to say is that they handled virtually every type of timber product. Their substantial works employed much local labour; country craftsmen of the finest order. They also gave employment on a jobbing basis to self-employed timber fellers who felled by hand using axe and cross-cut saw - no chain saws in those days! - timber sought out and purchased by them over a widespread area. They offered a timber service which, as demonstrated already, included all

21

manner of items made from wood - some manufactured by their own direct labour force, whilst others made by local craftsmen were factored. However, a major concern for which they were famous and which did not feature upon their local advertising, and which had a major impact upon the canal, concerned their extensive fleet of canal barges. These they manufactured themselves over a period of many years, which they launched sideways into the water from their own canal frontage. Many of these found lasting fame within the history of the canal, their names like those of their captains becoming almost legendary. Perhaps the most famous being the above mentioned 'Unity' under Captain William Harding, whilst others rejoiced in names such as: Speculator, Endeavour, Peel, Kennet, Manwell, Perseverance, Cornflower and Jane, whilst their captains, several of whom served in the capacity for many years, were named amongst others George Harris, James Sweet, H. Hendon, John Aldridge, Henry Bright, Thomas Powell and F. Wheeler. That this firm and their barges contributed to the viability of the canal is beyond question, as many cargoes either originated from their premises or else were destined for it, and in so doing they played their part well in keeping this lovely stretch of commercial waterway long after the nearby railway competition had blighted its very existence.

A measure of the diversity of cargoes carried on the canal can best be gleaned by reference to the "rates of Tonnage" poster dated as "commencing December 1st 1836". This specifies tariffs for goods carried "on the Inland Navigation between Bristol and Reading by the Kennet and Avon Canal and Rivers Kennet and Avon communicating with the Thames direct to London". It goes on to list such items as: clay, chalk, flints (for potteries), gravel, manure of all kinds, marble, road materials of all kinds, hay, pipe clay, sawdust, stone, tan, bricks, lime, coloured earth, grindstones, millstones, rods and rough sticks, smart hoops, tiles and tin plates, bark, cattle, English timber, fruit, hurdles and vegetables, coal, coke and culm, corn, flour, cake, malt, meal and seeds, bacon, eggs, butter …. and so the list goes on - a veritable catalogue of almost unimaginable variety.

Incidentally - before leaving the canal and Messrs Robbins, Lane and Pinnegar, I record that they operated a fleet of steam engines over a period of many years. These were occupied almost exclusively in hauling the round timber to the saw mill. I believe them never to have used more than two engines together at any one time in their history. The Road Locomotive Society lists them as having owned a total of seven engines, commencing with an Aveling and Porter 6 hp single cylinder traction engine No 2504 of 1890. I believe the final pair working to have been both 5 ton steam tractors purchased new from manufacturers Messrs Brown and May of Devizes, namely: On 1st January 1909 No 8071 'Progress' and in August 1912 No 8728.

The launching of the barge 'Diamond' at the premises of its manufacturers Messrs. Robbins, Lane and Pinnegar.
(Photo courtesy of the Kennet and Avon Canal Trust)

23

CHAPTER V

Having made but brief mention of the Great Western Railway in the penultimate paragraph of the preceding chapter, I feel it pertinent to this story to outline a little of the layout and role of that form of transportation which existed nearby the Wharf Farm at that time - which was considerable. Firstly, it is important to comprehend that the G.W.R. in its final and fondly remembered form, did not in fact start out as such, even though the conception of its brilliant engineer Isambard Kingdom Brunel was to join the capital city to the far west. This was achieved in stages spanning several years and was finally to come about by the amalgamation and taking over of a number of small independent railway companies. Thus we find that by the end of the year 1847, the line from London to the west terminated at Hungerford.

On the 13th August 1859 the independent Berkshire and Hampshire Extension Railway Company - largely supported by the G.W.R, proposed that a line be constructed from Hungerford to Devizes. This was to be constructed to Brunel's broad gauge pattern of 7' 0¼" to be single track and to largely follow the route of the Kennet and Avon Canal. This railway company had as its first chairman the second Marquess of Ailesbury, the same Frederick George Brudenell-Bruce - John Fall's employer whose ardent support for the extension of the railway system was invaluable to their cause. This line opened on 11th November 1862 through to Devizes.

A small station named Savernake was built adjacent to the village of Burbage, being thought sufficient for the townspeople of Marlborough - several miles distant, a fact which left them sorely disgruntled. From its outset this new line was worked by the G.W.R. until in August 1882 the whole concern became vested in the G.W.R. proper. In that same year a small interchange station, having a siding, a run through goods shed and cattle yard was constructed at Burbage Wharf, immediately in line with and alongside the canal wharf. This was never intended for passenger use, being solely for the interchange of canal and railway traffic - presumably by manual and horse power! However, I suspect this to have not been very convenient as to reach one from the other necessitated using the road bridge over the canal - a detour of several hundred yards. The large goods shed also, like the wharf crane (which still survives) remained as a significant landmark to the former usage of this immediate area until quite recent times.

The above however, was by no means the only railway activity in the vicinity of Wharf Farm - far from it. In the year 1836 the merchants of Manchester proposed the construction of a railway line to form a through route and direct link between their city and the port of Southampton. This

Burbage Wharf November, 1994. Note the restored wharf crane.

was to be achieved, like the G.W.R. itself by linking together several smaller railway companies, and by the construction of a railway where previously none existed - to become known when later completed as The Midland and South Western Junction Railway covering a route which extended to 95 miles. Nevertheless, as sound a scheme as it was envisaged, forty years were to pass before any appreciable part was completed - this being the Swindon, Marlborough and Andover railway, a single track line which joined all three towns. Inevitably, innumerable difficulties were encountered, not the least being at Savernake, where a junction was to be constructed to allow these cross-country trains to run eastwards along the metals of the previously mentioned Berks & Hants Railway before heading southwards towards Andover. Nevertheless, this section finally opened for traffic on 5th February 1883. This date was soon followed by the opening of the Swindon and Cheltenham Extension Railway which allowed the northern route to be completed by running on to Manchester via existing lines. Similarly from Andover by obtaining running orders over London and South Western Railway metals into Southampton - the dream of the promoters of their cross-country line was finally realised.

The projected prosperity for their enterprise however, was sadly not to transpire as from the time of its inception until final closure, only the extensive military activity associated with the first world war, and subsequent building work at the garrison town of Tidworth and a few other sites provided a much needed but short-lived boost to the company's fortune - it finally being absorbed into the G.W.R. on 29th October 1923.

Also the original Savernake station mentioned above was connected in 1882 to the town of Marlborough by a branch line which terminated at the original station in a bay platform. A further short line was constructed along the contours of the forest, passing, for some of its length, through a tunnel cut deep into the chalk hillside then emerging to pass alongside the fields of Wharf Farm before running into a new station called Savernake High Level. So finally on 26th June 1898 the town of Marlborough had its long hoped for direct rail link to the ever expanding world.

Thus it can be seen, that with all the great activity that was inevitably connected with this rapid railway expansion programme; its original construction and then in the case of the G.W.R., upon the outcome of 'The Gauge War' and its consequent re-alignment to standard gauge of 4' 8½" in 1874 - that the whole area around the Wharf at the time of John Fall's arrival as tenant (the same year of 1874), must have been one of total hustle and bustle. The canal was in great use; the railways and associated buildings were being constructed, altered and extended. Many thousand labourers were undoubtedly active in the area, a time of great activity for sure, but also one undoubtedly of great vigilance. What a time indeed for a man to seek to establish himself. As he looked out from his Wharf farm house he must oft-times have mused that he was content - his role as Wharfinger was already well established and invaluable to the local community, and his farm, even though his land was dissected by railway lines was now assuming an orderly routine. However, he had one other enterprise which was expanding to further occupy his waking hours, which also demanded his commitment - that of being a Steam Ploughing Contractor.

Approaching the end of a pull, Bill Fall eases the regulator, watching carefully as the plough comes close. *(Photo courtesy Cecil Brown)*

CHAPTER VI

At the commencement of Chapter IV I made mention of John Fall's interest in Wharf Farm centering around three items - firstly the farm itself, then the wharf, and thirdly steam threshing contracting. I stated that I have heard mention that the previous tenant, prior to 1874, had conducted this trade from those premises - but without proof. From that date onwards however, the family's activity in the field of steam engine ownership and operation is recorded and can be substantiated without question. Barely two years after his arrival at Burbage Wharf in April 1876, he purchased a brand new pair of 14 hp single cylinder ploughing engines from their makers John Fowler and Co of Leeds. These being manufacturer's numbers 2895 and 2896, the only note in Fowler's register of that date being that they were fitted with eccentric coiling gear and had 30 strand wire rope.

This same register does not record what, if any, new implements were supplied at the same date, however it is logical to suppose that this would have been the case, as engines on their own are useless without their implements, unless of course already existing on the farm. As previously referred to, there is now some speculation as to steam threshing contracting having been conducted from Wharf Farm, prior to the commencement of this tenancy - but no mention has been made of steam ploughing. I am therefore of the opinion that this order to Messrs John Fowler would have been for a complete set of engines and tackle, namely Nos. 2895/6 a plough, cultivator, drag harrows, living van and water cart. These items would in all probability have been delivered by rail - as was the custom of the day - to the nearest station having a suitable railhead, in 1876 - most likely Savernake. Further knowledge that implements were included in this order, comes from a most unexpected source, and provides for me at least, conclusive proof. Sometimes the budding historian receives a stroke of luck!

For me, this manifested itself, in one of the small handful of items from that period which has survived in the family ownership - and which has been made available to me. This being a relatively small stiff brown cardboard covered book, of a convenient size to slip into a jacket pocket, and is no less an item than John Fall's 'acreage book'. Produced in modern cheque book style with a tear off section, each page of which is headed "Burbage Wharf, Marlborough". The first counterfoil entry, presumably in his own hand records: No.1 JULY 1885. MR HAINES, ADDRESS... EASTON. ACRES. PLOUGH AT . . .
CULTIVAT (WITHOUT THE 'E') 8 ACRES AT 14/- (TOP) ABOVE WHICH IS WRITTEN 'TWICE' EQUALS £5.12.0. Interesting though this undoubtedly is, the more so, is countersigned No.2. DATED SEPTEMBER 1885 FOR MR HAINES OF EASTON again, where 24 ACRES WERE PLOUGHED ONCE AT 14/0 PER ACRE = £16-16- , TOGETHER WITH 17 ACRES CULTIVATED ONCE AT 8/- PER ACRE = £16-16- , which also bears a handwritten

note of 'Coal and Water' whilst opposite is noted coal for the job in hand being provided on no less than three occasions, firstly in a 4 ton lot, then subsequently $1^{1}/_{2}$ tons and 15 cwt to make a total of $6^{1}/_{4}$ tons.

This fascinating book about which more will be written later, covers the period from that first entry of July 1885 until July 1897 and contains two hundred leaves. It is the more remarkable in that it clearly demonstrates the owner's faith in his ability to find sufficient work in his immediate locality to warrant his purchase of this equipment and the extensive outlay that it represented. To have filled a book of two hundred pages, some of which are entered PAID, whilst the majority are marked ENTERED, in a little over a decade represents a considerable amount of work undertaken, covering many hundreds of acres; especially when one considers that many entries, particularly in relationship to cultivating, are overwritten TWICE.

What is even more remarkable, and here I digress, is that the era in which John Fall should seek to establish himself as a farmer and steam ploughing contractor was marked nationwide as the beginning of a sustained and increasing depression in agriculture. This started almost simultaneously with his arrival at the Wharf. A fundamental change in English agriculture came about following a long period of steady prices which came to an end in the mid-1860's, and was marked by a persistent decline in the price-level for cereals from about 1879 to 1894 and which remained thus for ten years longer. In turn, unable to reap a satisfactory return for their corn, farmers increasingly moved away from the plough towards grassland. This was sadly also in many cases not to be the panacea that they had hoped for, as a succession of wet years coupled with the cattle plague of 1879, further contributed to the decline, rapid in many instances, of a great number amongst the farmer community. Some idea of the effect and depth of the depression in English agriculture at that time, can be gauged in the knowledge that during the period 1875 - 1917, which latter date includes the jump associated with the outbreak of The Great War, some 3,121,877 acres went out of cultivation. In England alone as a whole, the proportion of land under the plough fell from 56 per cent of the total farming area in 1875 to 42 per cent in 1928 - a decline which understandably was not uniform across the country. There in that last sentence, lies perhaps the reason why John Fall's new venture was from the outset, so successful and bucked the common trend. He undoubtedly had gambled upon his knowledge of the area in which he lived, and in which he intended to trade as virtually all of his prospective customers, both then at the outset of his enterprise and until its cessation two generations later - lived and farmed in the Vale of Pewsey. This lovely area of central southern England is renowned for its fertility - picturesque valley floor of rich dark soil, sheltered on its northern flank not only by Savernake Forest but the Marlborough Downs, and from sweeping cold rain clouds from the south west by the mass of Salisbury Plain - whilst standing guard over its eastern end the high chalk hills of the Berkshire/Hampshire boundary keep the chill winds at bay.

If further evidence is needed to illustrate the parlous times through which British agriculture was passing then it comes from an altogether unexpected source; yet one which also clearly illustrates that in every sphere of life and in every context there is always an exception to the rule. During every age there have been those, often very few in number, who either by their foresight or entrepreneurial skill have risen above their fellow men, most usually succeeding against the common trend, often with spectacular results. Down through the ages, agriculture has had its fair share of such champions - one such being George Baylis.

George Baylis was born near Pangbourne, Berkshire in 1845, the son of a farmer, who before going to the city to study law, spent a year on the family farm. Articled as a solicitor, he soon became disenchanted with city life, and yearned to return to the land, which he did after appealing for cancellation of his articles to the Lord Chancellor in 1866. At the age of twenty-one, he took a farm of 240 acres at Bradfield where he set about farming in the orthodox way - losing £600 in his first six years - which drove him in desperation to explore an alternative way of using his land to produce a profit. Applying his undoubted clever brain to the problem, he considered the advice emanating from the experiments of Lawes and Gilbert of Rothamstead who had proved that by the use of artificial manures - then in its infancy - cereal crops could repeatedly be grown on even marginal land, without the need for livestock, root crops, sheepfolding, and expensively hauled and spread farmyard manure.

Determined to put this theory to the test which was revolutionary in context in 1875 he purchased the 400 acre Wyfield Manor Farm at Boxford, near Newbury for £15,000, financed by two mortgages - he having no capital. Abolishing all livestock, he envisaged a programme where fertility of the land was to be maintained by the use of artificial fertilizers; the land kept clean by the aid of bare fallows; humus to be retained by ploughing-in all stubbles and clover root, and where the total production of grain straw and clover hay was to be turned directly into cash.

Devising a six year rotation of corn, fallow, corn, clover, corn and fallow, his gamble paid off with unbelievable success. His low cost system, which occupied his labour force the whole year through; from after harvest, with the sowing of autumn corn on the fallows and clover stubbles; through the dead season, with threshing, baling hay, and ploughing corn stubbles; to sowing spring corn. Then came the cultivation of other fallows and haymaking until the first harvesting of the earliest sown winter barley commenced. His system was not burdened with the cost of maintaining costly livestock housing, or of their constant demands of labour for feed, bedding or 'mucking-out', and from the outset proved rewarding. So much so that during the next fifty years he was to take on - much of it by freehold ownership - vast tracts of land in his native Berkshire, as well as large areas of adjacent farmland in neighbouring Wiltshire and Hampshire. By 1917, this revolutionary, perceptive farmer had so gone against the prevailing tide during an era of almost unprecedented decline that he was to become the nation's largest arable farmer, owning or occupying no less then 12,140 acres. At that date, with almost two further decades of limited expansion and consolidation still to be enjoyed, he had purchased no less than 6,150 acres at a total expenditure of some £98,300! When one considers that at the outset he was almost in penury and that this success was achieved against a background of widely fluctuating cereal prices, most often in a downward spiral - then one can have nothing but great admiration for this remarkable man. He was, without doubt, one of the great agriculturalists of his age, and as previously mentioned, one of a very select band of revolutionary farmers, whose inventiveness and foresight have blazed a trail down through the years for others to follow and adapt to their particular circumstances as time dictates.

It is remarkable that central southern England should seem to possess more than its share of these gentlemen, who down through time have written their own pages of agricultural history. I record Jethro Tull whose invention of the seed drill and experiments with plant breeding and horse hoeing lived and farmed near Hungerford in Berkshire. Then in the early decades of this century in and around Wexcombe in Wiltshire, Arthur Hosier who, following his invention of the portable milking parlour (the Hosier Bail), successfully demonstrated that, by again using a low cost system, the fertility of the marginal land of the chalk hills of the area could be maintained and improved by cows in much the same way as George Baylis did with his style of cereal production. Again so successful was this system that, by the middle of the twentieth century, Arthur Hosier and his family were to farm many thousands of acres, and conclusively prove that, on much of this hitherto unproductive land, commercial dairying could be successfully accomplished. Roland Dudley of Linkenholt, a contemporary of Arthur Hosier, was a man whose mind and energies were focused on the increased mechanisation of agriculture, to the end that he possessed one of the very first combine harvesters to be used in this country, a peg-drum, side fed machine of American manufacture. Then too, Rex Patterson adapted the Hosier system of milk production to his particular taste, and became revolutionary with his great number of contract-milked herds of cows, each having a set number of acres, employing strip grazing, relying on self-fed silage for winter fodder made in due season by the use of his patented Buck Rake.

Returning to George Baylis, it is interesting to note that much of the land under his tenancy or ownership came about as a direct result of the farming depression at the time, some having been repossessed by mortgagees, other having been given up by its owner, some via bankruptcy, whilst much lay derelict unable to attract a tenant or freehold owner. In numerous cases he took over the tenancy for a few years and converted this to freehold ownership at a later date. At the height of his enterprise he employed year round, one hundred standard two-horse teams of heavy horses for ploughing, as well as owning his own set of steam ploughing tackle. The large acreage of many of his fields lent themselves to be more economically viable to this form of cultivation.

All of this then, is the background against which John Fall commenced his agricultural contracting business. From the outset this proved successful, sustained as he was by the farmers who sought to use his services being established in the fertile Vale of Pewsey - surely one of those small tracts of land which proved the exception rather than the rule.

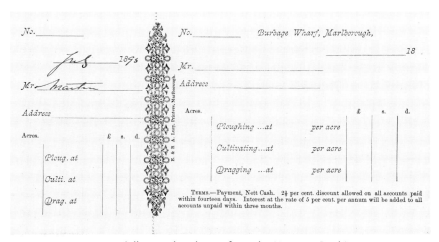

A partially completed page from the 'Acreage Book'

CHAPTER VII

By careful study of John Fall's previously mentioned first 'acreage book' an insight into the method of farming, and its rotation of crops towards the end of the nineteenth century can be formed.

With the exception of those fields adjacent to the farmstead, which inevitably would have been permanent pasture on a mixed economy farm, the remaining land would have been utilised upon a rotational system of cropping. In this way by interring the residue of some crops and by introducing on a regular basis those of leguminous nature i.e., sainfoin and clover, the fertility of the soil was maintained. This was immeasurably enhanced by the spreading of farmyard manure in due season - itself conducted upon a structured plan of fields in turn. The latter whilst undoubtedly the most potent of fertilizer available to the farmer of that era, inherently possessed the greatest obstacle - that being its ability to spread and propagate weeds, even though most often it would have been well matured in a "mixen" before being taken to the fields and spread. Nevertheless before the advent of chemical sprays one of only a few means of keeping weeds at bay and cleaning the arable acres was by cultivation and hoeing. The latter being extensively used in root crops providing a welcome source of labour for many a countryman and his family at regular intervals of the year, even if it was monotonous and back-breaking.

For the larger areas destined for cereals which it must be remembered were broadcast sown, repeated tilling with horse or steam cultivators was employed, either between crops or when the land lay fallow from one season to another. This method was extensively used to clean land that had become infested with couch grass, when the withered weed grass would be harrowed and hand raked up into manageable clumps to be burnt on the field, or else carted by horse to an odd piece of ground adjacent to the headland - there to be similarly destroyed by fire. Similarly a 'fake seedbed' was extensively used by farmers of that era in their battle with weeds in growing crops. For this method the land to be sown was prepared in the usual way - the seedbed being finely conditioned - then left for a few days. In this time the majority of the weed seeds would germinate and endeavour to take root. A swift passage with a light harrow followed which raked out the tender growing weed seeds, to be followed immediately by the sowing of the destined crop. The result being that the desired crop was now able to establish itself and grow up in advance of the weeds, which perforce were now much weakened and predominantly choked by its more vigorous neighbours. Accordingly it can be clearly understood that the cultivator and drag harrow were some of the farmer's most important implements and amongst the most frequently used.

It comes as no surprise then in thumbing the pages of John Fall's 'acreage book' to learn that virtually every entry contained on the counterfoil stubs refers to cultivating, most often over -written "twice" and on many occasions marked "three - times". Similarly 'Drag Harrow' entries are frequent in number, many also being recorded as "twice". It is also interesting to note that many of these operations were recorded as being undertaken in almost every month of the year, which in itself provides sufficient evidence of the efficacious use of fallow land combined with frequent cultivation. Naturally though, a significant increase is recorded for traditional autumn and spring sowing months, during the former, wheat would have been sown (spring sown varieties not at that time having been bred) whilst in the latter the sowing of barley would have been predominant.

It would appear that the farmers of this area at least, only spasmodically called in their local steam powered agricultural contractor to undertake ploughing for them. This I suspect was only the case when more permanent pasture land was to be brought into cultivation or as an expedient when, perhaps through a wet season, the work in hand had got behind schedule. It must however not be overlooked that these same farmers would have possessed their own teams of heavy horses who would most likely, even at the rate of an acre per day per team, as opposed to say 15-20 per day for the steam ploughs, have been able to plough their own stubble fields during the close season, utilising their own labour force, which had to be employed and paid for all year round. It is a well recorded fact that even at the height of the steam ploughing era only some $2^{1}/2$% of ploughed land was turned by steam the remainder being horse ploughed.

Before leaving the subject of this fascinating 'acreage book', I feel justified in noting for posterity, the rates then being charged for each operation conducted by the contractor over the twelve year period of its usage - i.e., July 1885 - July 1897. As previously mentioned ploughing commenced at 14/- (70p) per acre and would appear to have been reduced to 10/- (50p) per acre at the end of the period. Perhaps this was to encourage its usage or indicative of the severity of the depression then affecting the whole industry as outlined in the previous chapter.

The charge for cultivating commenced at 8/- (40p) per acre for a 'once-over' operation, with no reduction for either the second or third time over i.e., 16/- (80p) and 24/- (£1.20) per acre. Twelve years later the charge had risen to 10/-(50p) per acre, again with no reduction for additional operations. Drag harrowing is listed in the 'acreage book' as commencing at 5/- (25p) per acre for a single pass, 9/6d (45p) for "twice" reducing to 16/- (80p) for "four times over". The last recorded entry in the book for Drag Harrows is dated May 1897 and states that twenty-five acres were traversed twice for a Mr Cundell of Hungerford for £7-10-0d being 3/- (15p) per acre. Thus of all the operations carried out by 'The Falls' as contractors during

34

their first twelve years of establishment, only cultivating would appear to have significantly risen in price by some twenty per cent; whilst the charge for ploughing and drag harrowing had decreased.

Not only does this invaluable book provide the documentary evidence of contractors' rates as outlined above, during the closing years of the nineteenth century when the application of steam power on the land against all the odds, was in its ascendancy, but in the case of 'The Falls' provides a true picture of their travels during those times. Admittedly, by familiarity many of the counterfoils in the 'acreage book' only bear the briefest of details - such as the farmer's name; the address of the farm being most often only referred to by the name of the village. Nevertheless this is sufficient to reinforce my belief that this family's steam ploughing contracting business was as aforesaid largely confined to the Vale of Pewsey with only very occasional forays further afield, such as to the outskirts of the then small market town of Hungerford, just over the Berkshire County boundary. This is further borne out by the personal recollections of a number of elderly gentlemen with whom I have spoken, who witnessed this family's activities certainly from the early decades of this century until their demise.

In Chapters IV and VI, mention is made of the possibility of a previous tenant of Burbage Wharf Farm being engaged in steam threshing contracting, which is to date not proven. However, I record that in February 1892 John Fall purchased a new traction engine for just such a purpose. This was of Ransomes, Sims and Jefferies Ltd manufacture from Ipswich - numbered 8746 and named by its owner 'Savernake', later under the 1921 Registration of Vehicles Act to be accorded the Registration HR4996. This transaction is recorded in the manufacturers 'Register of Engines Sold' of the appropriate era, and states that the customer's order number 8450 was for a 7 hp traction engine, which bore the factory number 5264 stamped upon its boiler; was dated 2nd February 1892 and more significantly the customer's name is given as John Fall and Son. This first mention of the 'and Son' refers to the youngest of his five children George Mason Fall who was now twenty-six years of age, and destined ere long to carry on the family firm. I speculate that the owner intended to capitalise upon his friendships forged with his steam ploughing customers and sought to increase his business by offering these farmers an additional service. That his thinking was undoubtedly soundly based is borne out by the fact that, during the years that followed, his successors were to purchase a further two traction engines, and carry out steam threshing contracting continuously for nigh on the next sixty years. Sixty years which spanned two World Wars and during which the sight of their engines and threshing drums, like their steam ploughing tackle, would become so commonplace in their neighbouring village that it hardly drew mention - save the remark "I see old 'so-and-so' has got Falls thresher in again!"

However at the time of delivery of the first threshing engines John Fall had a little time left to him to further establish himself and family as farmers, wharfmasters and agricultural contractors trading out of Burbage Wharf. Time in which he took on the agency of Little and Ballantyne - the seed merchants of Carlisle, a connection which he most probably had forged during his years spent previously, when employed by the second Marquess of Ailesbury upon his Yorkshire estates. A role that caused him and his subsequent heirs to be listed in contemporary issues of Kelly's Directory as Commission Agent, as also was he noted as assistant overseer. Time was afforded him, to uphold the tradition of respected successful farmers of his day - which then he surely was - by joining the 'B' Company of the Wiltshire Yeomany.

JACK FALL on his own horse when with the 'B' Company of the Wiltshire Yeomanry.

CHAPTER VIII

John Fall was gathered to his fathers in the year 1894 (aged 64 years) to be succeeded as previously mentioned by the youngest of his three sons, the junior of his family of five children, George Mason Fall. John's eldest son - whose name was also John was, in the custom of the day, affectionately known as Jack. He however bore not only his father's christian name, but also that of his mother's maiden name having been christened John Ward Fall. He had by this time married and already moved away to premises in the nearby market town of Marlborough, known locally as 'The Wagon Yard' from where he also operated a set of threshing tackle. He did not, I believe, take any further interest in the affairs of the firm started by his father and now carried on by his brother. Nor did second son William who had moved away to employment in an outfitters shop in Bristol.

In the late 1890's George Mason Fall married Sabina Maud Guyatt of Shalbourne Manor in a service at St Mary's, Shalbourne, returning to the home of his widowed mother, there to resume his duties as head of the firm. It was here, just after the turn of the century, that his family of five - the same number of children as his parents - were born; firstly twin girls Doreen and Margery - January 8th 1902, to be followed by three sons Jack (1903), Harry (1906) and Bill (1912). I feel it worth noting here, that George's wife Sabina was the sister of Jack's wife Nellie - the connection between these two families being strengthened yet further by George's sister Annie - who married his wife's brother Harry Guyatt, thus these two families were unusually linked three times; i.e., two Fall brothers marrying two Guyatt sisters, whilst one Guyatt brother married one Fall sister! A strong relationship indeed, and one that would have undoubtedly made, in its forging, for very many journeys by pony and trap between the two villages!

Notwithstanding all this, George's hand on the tiller is clearly evident, as the writing in the 'acreage book' records; entries being made though similar in style and with a quill, but of a different hand. In Chapter VI I made first mention on the few surviving artefacts from this period being made available to me - one the 'acreage book', already dealt with. However interesting though that undoubtedly is to the historian of matters agricultural, another book survives from that same era and is of equal importance, as it relates, not like the former to acreages tilled and charges made by the contractor for services rendered - but to the employment of his labour force and to the level of wages paid to each for his service. This fascinating book, which undoubtedly was purpose made for the job in hand, is of exercise book size and like the aforementioned is covered in stiff brown mottled cardboard. It has two distinct sections, being effectively two books in one - with a blank section a third of the way through. From that point

1896	May 18 to 23				£	s	d
	Spackman	ı ı ı ı ı ı	6	2/	12		
	Dobson	ı ı ı ı ı ı	"	"	12		
	Coyn Boy	ı ı ı ı ı ı	"	/6	9		
	Wells	ı ı ı ı ı ı	"	1/9	9	6	
	Fisher	. . . . . .					
	Bowles	ı ı ı ı ı ı	"	/10	5		
	Taylor	ı ı ı ı ı ı	"	1/8	10		
	Sherwood	ı ı ı ı ı ı	"	2/4	14		
		Entered to Cash Book			3	11	6

Jackets lent 1/0 Fisher 1s Paid May 23

May 21 Fisher 1/2 " Butter /6 P.
" " Milk /3 P.

Extract from the 'Falls' Acreage Payment Ledger

onwards to the end it is titled 'Labour Book', and commences on a weekly basis to list out the names of those employed with the number of days each man worked, marked by a succession of ticks it gives the rate of pay of each employee and the total of wages paid. This is a fascinating window into past rates of remuneration for those engaged in steam powered agricultural contracting, made all the more so by the date of the first entry - December 31st - January 5th 1895. - the first year of George Mason as head of the firm!

The front section of the book becomes an 'Acreage Payment Ledger', where under a separate page titled for each employee and covering most often a year's span, the cash paid to each man as a bonus for acreage covered is recorded. These pages also reveal other interesting items, such as any goods received by the employee during that period, or the reimbursement due to him for any out-of-pocket expenses - all of which are detailed against the rate of bonus for each of the tillage operations undertaken by him, multiplied by the total of acres covered. This is then effectively a once-a-year 'settling up' of account on both sides, for employer and employee.

This ledger also reveals startling evidence of the loyalty paid to and shown by employer and employee alike, this has ever been so in agriculture where, oft-times, farm employees have served one family for a great number of years; often through more than one generation. Service which today rightfully continues to be marked not only at the very highest level by long-service awards being presented by The Royal Agricultural Society, but also in many instances by other provincial societies. This ceremony which is afforded due reverence is highly regarded, and is one of the highlights of any show. The era of steam power in agriculture is no less marked, for this especially amongst the steam engine drivers, where in many instances the length of service rendered by an individual has become legendary. 'The Falls' enjoyed this same brand of loyalty which is well documented in their 'Labour Book'.

As aforementioned the first entry is dated December 31st to January 5th 1895 and continues uninterrupted until June 12th - June 17th 1899 some four and a half years later. For the first few weeks the number of employees was recorded as six rising to nine by March, as presumably men were taken on for spring cultivations with a similar drop back most years to six for the close winter season. Throughout the period of the book, the rates of pay would appear to have remained constant i.e: 2/- (10p) per day for an engine driver: 'Cultivation man' 1/6 (7½p) per day; whilst another, most likely the ploughman received 1/8 (8p) - 1/10 (9p) per day - with the 'van boy' receiving 1/- (5p) per day. Thus it was G.M.Fall's first weeks wages bill entered in his ledger stood at £2. 19. 6d. (£2.98)! This was the pattern throughout the life of this 'labour book', the final weeks entry of which records that his outgoing to the nine men, at that time in his employ stood at £4. 6. 0d. Consistently recorded beneath the weekly details throughout the ledger, are

Spachman 1896

Extract from the 'Falls' Labour Book

further entries; e.g., on 21st May 1896 one by name of Fisher was noted as having half a pound of butter value 6d (2½p) and milk at 3d (1½p). However for several years the note that "Yeats lent 1/2" (one shilling and two pence) (6p) per week is recorded!   As regards the aforementioned loyalty of service, one by name of Spackman - an engine driver is listed almost from the first entry to the last, as also is Witts - whilst the entry accorded to 'Cultivation Man', 'Cook' or 'Van Boy' speak for themselves! Most often itinerant labour that 'followed - the - plough' in the case of the men, whilst 'Cook Boy' was just that, oft-times a junior of some local large family.

The front section of this same book as previously outlined contains the 'Acreage Payment Accounts'. The first entry being for the year 1895 and is again headed 'Spackman' - the aforementioned engine driver. Commencing on March 30th it is noted that he received five shillings (25p) as an advance from his acreage bonus payment.   Then in monthly order are other payments listed through to February 10th the next year. Similarly there are notations of him having received an allowance of coal (during the winter months), an entry for November 11th states 2 cwt of coal at 2/2, whilst one for November 18th is for 3 cwt at 3/3 with occasional others through to the end of the accountancy period - in total 21 cwt.   All this is brought together in a column on the right hand side which states that during the year he had taken part in cultivations covering 1,267 acres for which his bonus was 3d an acre equalling £15. 16. 9. Similarly drag harrows are listed as being 140 acres at the same bonus rate of 3d equalling £1.15.0. Ploughing being set at only 44 acres for which his bonus entitlement was 14/8 or 4d per acre. This tallied up at £18.6.5, from which sum his monthly advance as aforementioned and his purchase of coal amounting in total to £14. 12. 9 was deducted. This left a balance in his favour of £3.13.8 which was paid to him on February 18th 1896 surprisingly by cheque.

The next page deals, in similar style, with one named Dobson - the other engine driver - who had, like Spackman, received monthly payments on account, but who had not received any coal. Therefore the cheque paid to him on February 18th 1896 was considerably enhanced, being £9. 3. 5 - the acres and bonus payment being constant to both men, who it will be recalled at that time drove the only pair of single cylinder ploughing engines in the Falls' ownership.

The third page for that same year of 1895, is headed 'Witts' - another long time employee as mentioned in the previous chapter.   He presumably was the only other significant member of staff being undoubtedly the head plough and cultivation man; other employees such as second ploughman and van boy being in all probability casual labour, as was then the norm. This fascinating account book reveals that his acreage bonus payments were significantly less than that of the engine driver, remaining constant at 1d per acre for every type of operation undertaken.   He received only four

41

payments in advance throughout the year totalling £1. 7. 0, his final settling up payment - again on February 18th 1896 being for the sum of £4. 13. 11. This like the engine driver's was unusually paid to him by cheque - which I speculate called for some concern, as those engaged upon the land a century ago were unlikely to have bank accounts. Most likely this was changed for cash at the local hostelry, whilst it was still warm, several pints of ale being consumed during the time the transaction took place!

These three aforementioned pages then, set the pattern for the front portion of this invaluable account book. For it to have survived is fortunate indeed. It records not only the number of employees engaged by this family of agriculturalists, the hours they worked, the remuneration received by them for their labours - in itself an historical record from a previous century; but it goes on to record also, by a tally of the bonus payments per acre due to each main employee year on year, a total for each year of their entire steam contracting business showing the number of acres ploughed, cultivated and drag harrowed for their respective clients.

As an interesting aside, all these subsequent pages not only list the names of other employees from time to time but also record other purchases besides that of coal being made from their employer. It is a well documented fact that the diet of those living close to the land in days gone by was, to say the least, basic, therefore it comes as no surprise to learn that by far the most frequent entry in the ledger was for bacon, priced in 1896 at 8$1/2$d per lb. Numbered amongst other entries around the turn of the century are pork at 6d per lb, a head (presumably a pigs) at 6d, 2 rabbits at 1/6 and cheese (copious amounts) at 7$1/2$d per lb. These items, supplemented by bread and potatoes most likely, would have been the staple diet of those hard worked men - all washed down by large quantities of tea, brewed in a kettle, and drunk, each in turn from a small pudding basin. It is not surprising therefore that a welcome relief to this stark regime was sought from any handy Public House, when passed by in moving from farm to farm.

Before leaving the subject of the ledger, and in relationship to the long service of employees as mentioned in the previous chapter, I note that in the year 1900 the first reference is made to 'Spackman Son' who was employed as one of the gang. His acreage bonus payments covered 1007 acres of cultivating and 78 acres of drag harrowing for which his settlement payment, less monies received on account, amounted to £5. 12. 10. I specifically mention this because Isaac Spackman, named after his father, never sought employment with any other, commencing his employment with the family straight after leaving school aged twelve. He stayed with the 'Fall Family' and worked for them for the whole of his working life, a further sixty-two years, staying with them right through two world wars until after all steam related operations had ceased, when he filled his time out with general farm work. In all that time he lived in the village of Ogbourne St George - north of Marlborough, and walked the ten miles or so to work.

He never possessed a car or learnt to drive - save for steam engines! I am told that sometimes he would walk in to Marlborough and catch the train to Burbage Wharf if convenient - but at other times when the engines were out on contract work, he would walk out in the early hours of Monday morning (carrying his week's provisions) to wherever they happened to be, staying in the ploughing van all week, and walk home again the following Saturday afternoon. Together, these two generations of father and son spanned the total years that 'The Falls' carried on business using steam as agricultural contractors - surely a great testament to masters and men alike, a service of such loyalty that it deserves to be recognised and recorded here in print for all time.

Extract from the 'Falls' Labour Book

CHAPTER IX

Pausing a while to recap upon this chronological study of the family, I record that as the first decade of the twentieth century unfolded, we find George Mason Fall well established as head of the firm. His steam contracting business consisted of the pair of John Fowler ploughing engines of 1876 and the Ransomes, Sims and Jefferies traction engine 'Savernake' of 1892. The Wharf, even though privately owned by the Marquess of Ailesbury's estate, continued to be busy, despite the fact that the Kennet and Avon Canal had, by now, been in the ownership of the Great Western Railway for a half century. This demanded much close attention by the principal of the firm, as did also his own farming enterprise, which at that time was centred on a dairy herd.

His family of five were now growing, schooling for them as youngsters taking place at St Katherines Church of England School - a tiny hamlet set deep within the nearby forest some four miles distant, to which they most often would be taken by pony and trap, especially in inclement weather; whilst in summertime this journey in both directions would oft-times be made on foot. Following St Katherines, their schooling continued at Marlborough Grammar school for all, with the exception of the youngest, Bill. He in due time boarded away weekly at Devizes — surely a measure of the family's growing prosperity. The daily journey to Marlborough for schooling now most often took the form of a train ride, up the branch line from Savernake station. Except that is for Harry, the middle son, who usually rode his horse, which he stabled for the day with his Uncle Jack at the Wagon Yard in Marlborough, which was situated alongside the main London Road opposite the Five Alls public house and not but a stone's throw from the Grammar School. However, he was the naughty one, or so I have been told, who was known to have hidden his school books in the trunk of the famous, centuries old, 'Big Bellied Oak' - lying beside the main road nearby the hamlet of Cadley - and rode off to follow the hunt!

The 'boys' days at grammar school also resulted in them making many friends, especially amongst their more town-dwelling contemporaries, who enjoyed visits to the farm. Perhaps the knowledge that their friends' twin sisters would be present encouraged this closeness. However, many happy long summer days were spent in one another's company at the wharf, the visiting boys spending much of their vacation down on the farm, during which their accommodation was an old ploughing van. This influx of youth reached such proportions that 'the Wharf' was able to mount its own football team - of which their mentor George Fall was particularly fond and proud. They 'took-on' local village sides, a measure of success being theirs - a prized photograph remains of this heady era.

Marlborough Grammar School friends with their holiday accommodation at rear. JACK FALL in sidecar.

The first world war was marked by great activity - the canal being especially busy as the huge forest yielded up vast quantities of timber for the trenches and general war effort - as Harry remarked "the weighbridge at the granary was open day and night - a real busy place". This was also periodically used for weighing fat cattle which were driven on the hoof from neighbouring farms, weighed, then driven on to the cattle pens situated opposite the Savernake Forest Hotel, adjacent to the railway line where they were sold by auction.

This was a time also, when his eldest son Jack's education became severely interrupted as, often he was taken away from school to go as 'van or cook boy' for the ploughing gang - they being on what was termed essential war work. Jack now lived with the men in the van, and undoubtedly learnt his craft of engine driving and ploughing whilst so engaged; a norm in that sphere of activity - his lifetime's vocation being thus established. He never married, living his whole life at the farm where he was born.

It was around the time of the cessation of hostilities, that 'the Falls' established a milk round in the neighbouring village of Burbage in addition to the coal round. Coal which either was delivered to the wharf siding by rail or by barge to the canal wharf itself. It was the milk round which featured large in the life of second son Harry upon his leaving school aged fourteen. His task was to help hand milk the herd of shorthorn cows, necessitating a 6.45am start. After breakfast, he set off around Burbage in a pony and trap, where from ladle and churn he dispensed the milk to be back home by 11am sharp!

These long days of work were perhaps the halcyon days for this family firm, which might have hidden from their view the years of depression that so soon were again to overtake not only the agricultural community, but the entire nation, culminating in the general strike, mass unemployment and discontent. Once again, most likely, the fertile plain of the Vale of Pewsey and the almost closeted life of the largely family orientated villages within its bounds, led to an unnatural sense of well-being, and contributed in no small measure to the continued success of the family's enterprise.

This was soon to manifest itself in a most dramatic way, with the purchase of other engines to add to their stock of prime movers. The most notable of which being the purchase of a brand new set of Fowler ploughing engines and tackle in April 1919 from George Thurlow and Sons of Stowmarket in Suffolk - the main dealers for the products of the Steam Plough Works at Leeds. An order (No.K26580) was placed for them in the name of George Fall and Sons, a subtle change in the name of the firm which undoubtedly recognised the near approach to adulthood of 'the boys', Jack, Harry and Bill, then respectively sixteen, thirteen and seven years of age. This new set comprised a pair of compound ploughing engines, numbered consecutively by their makers as 15342/3 - subsequently accorded the Registrations of HR 3679/80. They arrived at Burbage Wharf, together with a new 11/13 tyne cultivator (order No. K26582) — tynes $4^{1}/4''$ x $1^{1}/4''$ x 10" No.1335 and a 7 ring land presser (order No. K26581) No. 13418. A formidable outlay of over two thousand pounds was a great statement of faith in their ability as a family to succeed. This undoubtedly was tempered by the fact that in purchasing their engines through Thurlows as agents, and not direct from John Fowler and Co, the transaction could be spread over a considerable length of time — they being well noted for their hire-purchase policy. A procedure which was not possible in dealing direct with that manufacturer, Messrs Fowler of Leeds being sufficiently large to seek payment in full upon completion of an order.

Other hard commercial factors would undoubtedly have played their part in George Fall's reasoning in deciding to buy a new set of tackle, which can be easily understood. Firstly the pair of single cylinder engines, with which his father John had commenced the family's undertaking, were by now forty -three years old, and of necessity well-worn, and probably in need of new boilers. Even though these could be readily obtained from various sources, not the least in that area, from the relatively nearby firm of John Allen of Cowley, for something in the region of £160-£200 each - the engines in themselves were old and single cylinder. Their tackle, for the most part, was similarly well worn and smaller than that which was currently available and in regular use with the more powerful compound engines. To have re-boilered these old engines was therefore not an economic proposition, given that their sale should provide a handsome down-payment in favour of their more modern counterparts.

It therefore comes as no surprise to record that an advertisement appeared in the May 23rd,1919 edition of The Marlborough Times - a full month after the arrival of the new BB1 engines - which stated :-

SALE ON WEDNESDAY NEXT

MARLBOROUGH, WILTS

Announcement of Sale of
STEAM PLOUGHING AND THRESHING
TACKLE, Etc, Etc

MESSRS, LAVINGTON & HOOPER are favoured with instructions to SELL by AUCTION at their SALE YARD as above (close to the G.W.R. and M. and S. W. railway stations),
ON WEDNESDAY, MAY 28th, 1919
at 2 o'clock in the afternoon.
A pair of 14 hp Ploughing Engines (Nos.2895 and 2896) with Tackle by Fowler, 7 hp Traction Engine by Wallis & Steevens, Two 6 hp ditto by Fowler, Threshing Machine by Tasker, Elevator by Maundrell, Straw Trusser by Howard, three Sleeping Vans, etc., etc., all of which is in good working order.
Catalogues may be obtained of the Auctioneers, Marlborough and Devizes

Thus the old original engines owned by the family from the commencement of their business were sold. Even though no contemporary report of the day's proceedings would appear to have survived, I have been told that the pair of ploughing engines and tackle were sold as one lot, with the exception of the ploughing van and drag harrows, which were retained at the wharf for further service, and were purchased by Mr Van der Stegen of Cane End, near Reading, a well-known engine collector at that time for £600. It will have been seen, that sold that day also was a 7 hp Wallis and Steevens traction engine of 1907 vintage No.2942 named 'Alfred the Great'.

I believe that engine to have come into the family's ownership some time previously to assist their Ransomes traction engine 'Savernake' in threshing duties, but which presumably at that time was considered expendable!

As an aside I mention that details of this undoubtedly sturdy engine are recorded in the surviving "Register of Engines" of its manufacturers Wallis and Steevens of Basingstoke. Page 147 of which lists the various drawings used in its manufacture, with details of any specific requirements by its first owner. It is in effect a catalogue of all the components used to make up and assemble the engine. It states for example the engine is to be equipped with - "A Wood Hood with sides dropped down and clothes box at back end and wrought iron standards". (In modern parlance, a cab with canvas side sheets, tool box at rear and supported on four iron stanchions). It continues; the engine is to be supplied with - two lamps on the smokebox and tail lamp on back of tank: Brass plate on Smokebox Door - "Alfred the Great". This interesting page also reveals the engine was leased upon its completion to one A E Smith of Kings Somborne, Hants. How long Mr Smith was the lessee I know not, nor the date upon which it came into the possession of the Falls. However, I believe it to have been purchased at the above-mentioned auction in Marlborough by Messrs Nash and Son, of Mildenhall (a small village situated only a couple of miles downstream on the river Kennet from Marlborough, and lying on the extreme northern boundary of Savernake Forest).

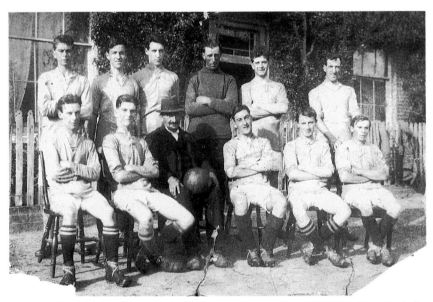

Burbage Wharf Football Team outside the farmhouse, GEORGE FALL holding the ball.

Regarding the remaining engines on offer that day, namely two 6 hp Fowler traction engines, I can only speculate .... I believe they could have been owned by George Mason Fall's eldest brother Jack - whom it is recalled did not take over the tenancy of the Wharf Farm upon the death of his father - the founder - John, but had already married, and moved away to Marlborough, to premises known then as 'The Wagon Yard'. The family told me, that "Uncle Jack carried out steam threshing contracting from there for a few years" - but they could not however recall the date his business ceased. Could it have been that he chose the moment of his brother's sale to divest himself of his engines and tackle? Especially as it is well documented that, at that time, steam engines were offered for sale almost wholesale, as the threat from the internal combustion engined tractors became a reality. It must also not be overlooked that Jack, unlike his younger brother George, was able to offer his clients only a service of threshing contracting, and hence could not rely so heavily upon the loyalty of his customers as he who could carry out cultivations as well. Similarly, the outlay necessary for those engaged in threshing contracting, was substantially less than that of the Ploughing Contractor, with the corresponding numerical supremacy of the former over the latter, with the end result that the viability of those singularly engaged in threshing duties was more easily threatened. However, at the time of writing I can only speculate on this, as regards Jack Fall, and the other engines on offer that day.

Nevertheless, now firmly re-equipped with a modern set of tackle, and with a younger generation of drivers coming along The Fall's field of activity would seem to have increased. I have heard mention of them carrying out cultivations as far east of their home base as the village of Inkpen, near Newbury, and west to out beyond the village of Lavington towards Westbury. Strange to tell it was only on occasional forays that they seemed to have crossed the A4 London to Bath road with their ploughing tackle. Similarly I record, the late Harry Fall telling me that their threshing round was much more confined to a smaller area of villages around Burbage - local farmers to whom they paid a visit on an annual basis

It was during these busy days that Harry had often to leave his cowshed and milk round duties to the cowman and help out with the threshing gang when they were short-handed. This in turn led to the family eventually relinquishing its milk round, preferring instead to deliver the milk to the Wiltshire Farmers Creamery depot at nearby Savernake station. This they did by pony and cart, the milk being transported in large 17 gallon conical churns. This creamery was a co-operative effort, as the name implies, by some Wiltshire farmers, and had small premises situated on an island site between the converging tracks of the Great Western Branch line to Marlborough and the more northerly line of the aforementioned Midland and South Western Junction Railway where they met - the former to join into the Great Western System; the latter to merge briefly with this before separating to head south towards Southampton. The establishment of this depot (close by a railhead) by local milk producers, followed a clear set pattern which existed around the country, in that the advent of reliable steam train haulage made it possible for milk to be delivered on a daily basis into the metropolis. Not so in days gone by, when cows roamed our cities and towns, the milkmaid with her yokes being a common sight. At the outset, the milk was transported in the churn, however this was soon superseded with the advent of the milk tanker wagon. The longevity and preservation of the quality of the milk was soon to be increased substantially by the pasteurisation process. Such a place as this was the Savernake station depot, which was a boon to the local farmers of the area, many from this fertile Vale of Pewsey, who still today carry on dairying as a mainstay of their enterprise. With the establishment of the depot at Savernake, for the first time in their history a sure market for their product was secured, without which, unless turned to butter or cheese, this essential to life could so easily be lost.

These premises at Savernake had commenced trading on April 1st 1919, following a meeting held at Burbage schoolroom on the tenth of January of that year. Under a heading of "Agricultural Co-operation" the local "Wilts, Hants and Berks County Paper, and Marlborough Times" of January 31st carried a contemporary report of that meeting. It states... "There was a good attendance of smallholders and others from the village .... together with the secretary and committee of the Wootton Rivers (a local village) Co-operative Society... Mr.Green, chairman of the Burbage Poultry Club was in the chair... The principle speaker was Mr. J.B.Foster, organising secretary for the "Southern Counties Division of the Agricultural Organisation Society"... In a clear and able manner he pointed out the advantages, both to buyer and seller, of co-operative trading and urged those present to link up with the Wilts Farmers... Mr.S.Corbett, Managing Director of the Wilts Farmers, was also present, and outlined the progress of the movement for opening a branch of the society at Savernake.... temporary premises for a general store are to be taken at once..."

The report goes on to conclude, that "arrangements have been made for opening a deposit for general stores at Westcourt Farm. A stock of foods will arrive almost at once, so that smallholders, pig keepers etc, will be able to obtain feeding stuffs, artificials etc almost immediately.... - It is understood that both the Burbage Poultry Club and the Wootton Rivers Society have decided to wind up their operations in order to encourage the success of the larger society in its new venture."

I have dealt at length with this newspaper account as in mentioning Wilts Farmers and the Wootton Rivers Co-operative Society, it clearly indicates that many local farmers in the area both at county and village level, had already banded together by that time, to seek out an advantage for themselves when trading as a body rather than individuals. This no doubt was

FOWLERS Nos. 3246/3247 of 1877 at Norton Bavant, Wiltshire, when in the ownership of G. F. Gauntlett. 14th July 1950.
(Photo Road Locomotive Society)

prompted by the realisation that with the Great War now mercifully over, the previous demand for their goods would soon evaporate - as also would the safeguard of their raw materials - even though severely rationed in time of war - be lost. Fears that were all too soon to manifest themselves. That their thinking was based on sound criteria was evidenced by the future growth of such co-operative societies, many of which survive to this day, the most notable in the south of England being the Southern Counties Agricultural Trading Society - S.C.A.T.S. for short. This continues to flourish, and operates not only a merchanting service to its farming clients, but has its own provender mills, besides a substantial number of renowned 'Country Stores', spread throughout its trading area of the counties from Kent to Devon, which offer a large range of goods to the wider populace.

The invaluable lists of the late Alan Duke, the former records officer of the Road Locomotive Society, state that around this time also - exact date not known - a further pair of John Fowler ploughing engines was purchased by the family firm. These were numbered 3246/7 of 1877, were single cylinder and accorded the Registrations under the 1921 Act of HR 3668 and HR 3669. They were believed to have been purchased from a Mr Wiles of Buttermere - a small hamlet, high on the chalk downs of the Hampshire/Wiltshire boundary. However by 1930 these had also been sold by 'the Falls' going to a local farmer G.F.Gauntlett of Norton Bavant a village on the south western boundary of Salisbury Plain nearby Warminster.

As the first quarter of the twentieth century drew to a close, it would appear that the Fall family were set fair amongst their contemporaries - their farm was prospering with a sure market for their milk. Their coal round, which in its heyday had been a considerable enterprise, in which they had supplied coal - several tons of it in each delivery, making many wagon loads, to Tottenham House, the magnificent mansion home of their landlord the Marquess of Ailesbury - as well as being the main suppliers to countless numbers of families within their immediate vicinity. Much of the coal destined for their delivery service arrived at the wharf by train, particularly during the latter era of that sphere of their business - and obviously so, after the canal ceased to be used for commercial traffic. Thus it was that on occasions following the chuffing and clanking associated with steam railway locomotive shunting, a cry would go up from the goods shed area across the void that spanned the canal to the Wharf "Mr Fall - yer coals come!" The wharf, even though the hectic days of the Great War Years had long since gone, still saw some, if only limited usage. This decline was more than compensated for by the strength of their steam ploughing and threshing contracting rounds, in which capacity they held a commanding position within their locality. However, as in all things, this was all too soon to change.

Burbage Wharf goods yard in the days of the Great Western Railway. Note the proximity of the farm in relationship to the building on the right.
(Photo courtesy of the National Railway Museum)

CHAPTER X

In the year 1925 George Mason Fall died, at the early age of fifty-nine years - a savage blow for the family. Like his father John before him - whom it is recalled died at the early age of sixty-four, his had been a busy life, perhaps leading to his early demise. He had come early to hold the reins of the family's enterprise, surely a very demanding role. This he had carried out in an exemplary manner guiding them all through the difficult times at the end of the previous century, when agricultural prosperity for all had experienced another of its dramatic downward spirals. He had coped with this, expanded their enterprise, and seen them safely through the turbulent years of the Great War. He had raised and cherished a family, brought stability to their home life, enjoyed their love and company and established himself as a much respected agriculturalist amongst his fellow men and been clerk to the local parish council - his demise was indeed a great loss.

George's death, as so often happens, led to major repercussions within the family - not the least being a change once more in the title of the firm; it now being known as Fall Bros. The tenancy of the farm was also changed with their landlord, the Marquess of Ailesbury's consent - to be held now in the name of George's widow Sabina together with that of her eldest son Jack. The late George's sister Cissie, in choosing to move back to their native Yorkshire home, caused for some concern, as she felt entitled to her share of her late father's estate. His widow, Sabina, who preferred to be known by her second name Maud, continued to live at home in the Wharf farmhouse, with her family; Bill the youngest by now having left school, fell in as odd man around the farm. Not long after this the dairy herd was given up, as the depleted family concentrated more on its agricultural contracting business.

Having worked for a couple of years or so as plough boy, occasional engine driver and general odd man around the farm, Bill left the family concern to seek more settled employment. This he found at the nearby Wiltshire Farmers Creamery at Savernake, staying there until it closed down circa 1935 - when the Newbury Creamery depot of The Milk Marketing Board commenced its operation. For a season he found his employ with the local well respected farming family of Gore, who farmed at Chaddleworth, near Newbury, for whom he drove their Fowler traction engine. With this and their 54" Marshall threshing drum (recently salvaged in derelict state for restoration!) he threshed their corn stacks and also carried out a small round of contract threshing duties for their farmer friends in the immediate neighbourhood. Following this, he joined the Milk Marketing Board at Newbury, during which time he married a dark haired, blue eyed Welsh girl by name of Susan Jones, whom he first met whilst working at Savernake, she

'END OF A JOB'. The pair of BB1's and cultivator in the corner of the field. c. late 1920's.

being employed at the nearby Savernake Forest Hotel. Following their marriage they set up their first home in Newbury, where their only son David William was born in 1948, later moving house to Headley, Leckhampstead and finally Great Bedwyn. Bill remained at the Newbury Creamery for twelve years, before leaving to take on the managership of the Newbury branch of Oakes Bros Ltd the local agricultural engineers: a position in which he was 'well-at-home' having been conversant with agricultural machinery since birth. He remained with Oakes Bros Ltd until his retirement in 1979 during which time he continued to earn the respect and friendship of all with whom he came in contact. It was during this time also that he found lasting pleasure, and made many more friends of all generations and from every walk of life, within the steam preservation movement. Sadly he died "before his time" in February 1984 aged seventy-two.

Back at Burbage Wharf.... Jack and Harry carried on, living with their mother and sisters Dolly and Molly. They worked as a pair when ploughing, each driving one of the BB1's. Sometimes however one by name of Ernest Hiscock who worked for them for a good number of years, mostly as ploughman, was paired with Harry - this was during the times when eldest son Jack was away on duty with the 'B' Company of the Wiltshire Yeomanry - to which he rode his own horse, following in the family tradition set by his father.

By the end of the 1920's presumably the venerable Ransomes, Sims and Jefferies traction engine 'Savernake' of 1892 had tired somewhat of carrying out single handedly the threshing round, as it had done since the sale of the Wallis and Steevens 'Alfred the Great' ten years previously. It was now joined in what I believe to be swift succession by the two final engines that were to make up the fleet of steam motive power accorded to the family. Namely, 7 hp Fowler traction engine No. 11814 of 1909 Registration MO2909 named 'Berkshire Tariff Queen' by its first owner Thomas N.Stephens of East Hanney and then perhaps an engine which was purchased in an attempt to further expand the threshing round, a Fowler compound class A9 traction engine No. 15378 on springs - supplied new in 1920 to the well-known agricultural engineering firm of T.Baker and Sons of Compton, who were local agents for Fowler, against order No.K 27499 for a Mr. Appleby of Woolley. This undoubtedly handsome engine was accorded the Registration BL8718 and went to the Falls as its second owner.

Jack and Harry carried on, both steam ploughing and threshing until the end of 1936, by which time as Harry recalled "modern tractors were coming in" - to such a degree that there was not enough work for all to live at home. He left on 1st January 1937 to commence his employment at the same Newbury Creamery depot of the Milk Marketing Board, as his younger brother Bill had before him - taking up the position in February of that year as Transport Manager. It was with this branch of agriculture - the Milk Industry - that this one-time milk boy was to stay employed for the

'BERKSHIRE TARIFF QUEEN'   FOWLER No. 11814 of 1909 an R Class traction engine, splendidly restored to original livery.
(Photo courtesy Roger Newbery, September 1985)

BILL FALL riding the plough at Manor Farm, Pewsey. c. mid-1920's.

remainder of his working life. 1937 was indeed to be a significant year in Harry's life, for on the eleventh of September he married Hilda (née Lloyd) at St. Nicolas Church in Newbury. His wife was a Great Bedwyn girl, born at The Three Tuns public house,and whose schooling was conducted in the village. Later her parents moved to become the landlords of The New Inn at Burbage, where she soon met up with the local farmer's son. However, their courtship was to be conducted over a considerable distance - for those days - as they again moved away to take up the tenancy of The Bricklayers Arms in Bartholomew Street, Newbury. Harry persevered - hence the wedding took place in that town's Parish Church, their first home being at 19 Priory Road, Newbury, where their only child John was born in 1940.

In 1943 Harry was promoted to the Milk Marketing Board's Regional Office in Reading (Region 8) to the position of assistant Regional Officer, a post he retained until taking early retirement in 1968, by which time he had made his home at Burghclere, near Newbury. It was from this bungalow, which he had largely planned and built himself, that he too in his retirement, like his younger brother Bill, would foray forth, to revel in the steam preservation movement, often when first retired to be found at the controls of an engine, especially if it was a traction engine or even more so a ploughing engine - manufactured by Fowlers! To see him thus ensconced was indeed a great sight - for here was a true professional at work, when man and machine were as one. He had a stance upon an engine; a presence, that my own late father also possessed, that comes to few; and one which is only borne of those 'old engine men who cut their teeth on these mighty machines'.

MR & MRS HARRY FALL married at St. Nicholas Church, Newbury, 11th September, 1937.

FOWLER BB1 of 1919 Driver ERNEST HISCOCK (right). Notice the bundle of old thatching spars on the front toolbox for 'lighting up' wood.

HARRY FALL on Fowler BB1 15343 of 1919, HR3680 at John Strong's Manor Farm, Pewsey, Wiltshire. c. mid-1920's.

CHAPTER XI

I know not the date of the cessation of steam as a motive power employed by 'the Falls' at Burbage Wharf, save that I believe steam ploughing contracting to have virtually petered out by the onset of the Second World War, with only a few notable exceptions. One of which involved Bill Fall, who was granted leave of absence for the requisite time from his employment at the Newbury Creamery to assist his elder brother Jack, in this 'essential war work'. The job in hand was to cultivate a fifty acre field at the hamlet of Marten, which lay adjacent to the A338 road nearby the Nags Head Public House some five to six miles distant by road from Burbage Wharf. Steaming away from the farm, just as dawn was breaking, they travelled to Marten and 'set to' to cultivate that field, returning home late that same evening. What makes this the more remarkable is that the field in question was cultivated twice over during that one long working day - a hundred acres covered; but in a day which included the wartime expedient of "Double Summer Time" - when the clocks were advanced two hours to make most use of the daylight hours. Notwithstanding this however, that particular day's toil was nevertheless a remarkable achievement which exemplified the commitment of the steam ploughing contractor.

However, it has again been widely documented that, for a fair number of steam ploughing contracting firms, the period of global hostilities 1939-45, with its consequent emphasis on Home Food Production, in themselves led to a 'second-coming' for this sphere of steam power. This is undeniably true, and was the salvation by which many fine engines and implements have survived to this present day. However, as has been documented, at Burbage Wharf the Fall family had become severely depleted by that time, two of the three surviving male members of the family having 'flown-the-nest' to seek their fortunes elsewhere.

I therefore believe I am correct in recording that only the latter two traction engines - the Fowler 'Berkshire Tariff Queen' of 1909 and the same maker's compound traction engine of 1920 were pressed to service for threshing duty, which in itself was to cease soon afterwards. Similarly, the Kennet and Avon Canal had suffered the ravages of time - the last recorded working barge having passed by the wharf in the year 1948. Subsequent to which some of the locks, their gates having almost totally collapsed, were bricked up in an attempt to contain the water and prevent flooding further downstream. Consequent to this was that the Wharfinger, remaining son Jack received no income from that portion of their former enterprise, even though he, like his father before him, continued to be affectionately referred to by local people as "the Harbour Master".

Having, during this narrative, mentioned if only briefly from time to time,

John Falls first-born children, the twins Molly and Dolly, I record that both girls found their lifetimes' vocation as schoolteachers. As aforementioned, their education was conducted firstly as infants at St. Katherines school, lying snugly within the forest, to be followed by Marlborough Grammar school - largely the same as their younger brothers. By the time of their leaving, they had decided to pursue a career as infant school teachers, and were given the opportunity of undertaking their training for this at Nottingham. However at that time the Great War was still raging in Europe, with consequent deprivation and uncertainty for this nation at home. Their father therefore decided that Nottingham was "no place for his girls", who returned to their old school- Marlborough Grammar - to learn their vocational skills. Like all others, their Alma Mater was short staffed and received them back - this time as junior members of staff - with open arms.

A few years later and now sufficiently accomplished to take up their new posts, the twins departed Marlborough to go their separate ways - Molly to teach infants in Wiltshire, Dolly to undertake the same duties in neighbouring Berkshire. For the greater part of her career Molly taught at the village of Easton Royal, a village that at one time had lain within the bounds of the forest of Savernake, and which was situated in the same fertile plain of Pewsey. She never married and lived at home at the wharf during all this time, in turn keeping house for her mother and brothers, until towards the end of their tenancy she remained solely to look after brother Jack. Following his demise and in her autumn years she took up residence in a warden controlled flat in Burbage - only a short walk away from her former home.

Twin sister Dolly left home in 1923 to teach at a succession of village schools to the north west of Newbury, out towards the Vale of the White Horse, namely Chieveley, Lambourn, Compton and Peasemore, taking lodgings at Leckhampstead. Whilst living in this village she met Albert Edward Deacon a master carpenter and wheelwright. They were married at St.Katherines Church "back home in the forest" on September 7th, 1940, following which they set up their first home in the village in which he plied his trade, at a little thatched cottage of venerable age -"all wattle and daub" known as 'The White House'. Here they lived until 1961 before moving to 'Chapeldene' - a cosy house constructed out of the former village chapel, where Dolly continues to live in her widowhood, her husband having died in 1964, some two years after she had retired from her profession. In retirement I am sure both ladies can look back satisfied in the knowledge that countless numbers of young children - all adults today - passed safely through their hands - most of whom, I am confident could look back upon their time spent under their care with gratitude and affection.

Not surprisingly then, that as the 1940's drew to a close the farming system at 'the Wharf' had radically altered - no more was there the need to feed a large family; a family so often swelled by visitors in former years -

Burbage Wharf (c. 1947) after all steam engine operations had ceased – the engines lying beside the canal wharf and in full view of the main road, becoming a familiar landmark to many passers by.

hence Jack Fall chose to devote several of his acres to growing potatoes. This, together with a rotation of arable crops, became the norm from that time onwards. In doing so he unquestionably became "the Potato King" of Burbage, a role that suited him well- for everyone roundabout knew him well - for had he not spent the whole of his life living at the wharf, and visited virtually every local parish and farm during his steam contracting days?

This then was the pattern that existed, at that once so busy place, when the late John Boughton of Amersham visited the Wharf in about 1947. He recalled that "he knew of Falls engines". John Boughton, later to be the managing director of the firm that bore his name; a firm that had grown up in unison with the development of the road steam engine, and had used vast numbers of the same in timber hauling, threshing contracting and road rolling operations. The firm was entrusted by the Colonial Development Corporation to purchase, refurbish and export two sets of ploughing engines and tackle to the Ground Nut Scheme in Africa. It was in this connection that he visited the Wharf. In his correspondence to me a month or two before he died on 13th July 1992 in his seventy-fifth year he continued "At the time there were two Fowler traction engines at Burbage, as I recall. One a Fowler compound with belly tank and solid fly wheel in the 15000 series; I would think it was a six horse power. The other a Fowler single threshing engine about a seven horse power, possibly in the 11000 series. The former had obviously stood for many years". He continued "I bought the engines (the pair of BBI's), together with the plough and what remained of the cultivator, for scrap price. The engines were not steamable as the tubes had rotted away and they were in a sorry state although basically sound in many ways."

These engines were subsequently collected by the late Jack Hardwick of Ewell, well-known engine dealers and scrap metal merchants, and returned to Boughtons works at Amersham. Here they were completely overhauled and restored to a high standard prior to being exported. The quality of this workmanship can be witnessed by reference to the photograph contained in this work which illustrates the right hand engine prior to despatch overseas. As an aside to this, I recall learning as a young man, that the African Ground Nut Scheme was an abject failure - in which much of the equipment sent out to it, was apparently never used! Could it possibly be that in some far off corner of that vast continent this once fine pair of engines lie quietly awaiting rescue?

Returning to John Boughton's letter, and his remembrance of his visit to the wharf nearly a half century ago - this contained startling information, and I believe one omission. Which is that at that time my records would indicate that the venerable Ransomes, Sims and Jefferies traction engine 'Savernake' was still lying there. The fine frontispiece photograph to this book taken around the time of John Boughton's visit, clearly shows three

JACK FALL – "THE POTATO KING OF BURBAGE" – taken at his clamp in the late 1980's.

JACK FALL shortly before his death in 1991.

FOWLER BB1 of 1919 – after purchase and overhaul by T. T. Boughton Ltd. – prior to shipment to African Ground Nut Scheme. *(Photo courtesy the late J. H. Boughton c. 1947. Original p.112 "Steam in the Veins" by J. H. Boughton)*

traction engines present - the second ploughing engine being at that time parked up behind the Granary building, and out of camera shot.

I deem it not unlikely that following 'Hardwicks' visit to the wharf to transport the BBI's to Amersham as described above, they returned at some later juncture to purchase the Ransomes and the compound Fowler for scrap? Again, I have no knowledge of this, but the demise of these two engines from 'the Falls' fleet is unrecorded, and as such the fate of this pair is open to conjecture. Should the above statement have any basis in fact, what is known is that the Fowler traction engine 'Berkshire Tariff Queen' of 1909 survived this clear out of engines, becoming the last remaining engine at the wharf subsequently being sold to the well-known firm of amusement caterers, R. Edwards and Sons of Swindon, in whose ownership it is recorded as "post 1950".

For those of my readers who are not conversant with road steam engine history, it might appear unusual for an amusement caterer to purchase, what was then a derelict traction engine. However, this is not the case, as Messrs Edwards in fact collected together, either by bulk purchase from other sources or as individual items, several dozen engines of varying types, which I am told they did in order to reduce them to scrap metal. This would have been undertaken during their 'close-season' of travelling - the winter months - as time and the price of scrap dictated. These engines were stored either at their yard in Ferndale Road, Swindon or else at a disused gravel pit near Fairford in Gloucestershire. I believe I am correct in saying that other more easily and less costly - in terms of 'cutting up' - items of scrap became available, with the corresponding result that a great number of their stock of engines survived. As they did so, so too did the preservation movement gather momentum from the early 1950's onwards which, now happily looked toward Swindon and Fairford for part of its source of engines. This quite quickly led to the value of these, by then derelict engines, becoming much greater than their scrap value, with the direct result that the vast bulk of them survived.

It is fair to say that, by this combination of circumstances, many fine engines - amongst which some very rare, and in a few instances the sole surviving examples of their type - exist today. For myself, in common with many other aspiring engine owners, I recall the excitement felt when visiting these places, where engines lay in great profusion. We mused over which one to purchase, then made 'tongue-in-cheek' offers to the late Bob Edwards, who received us with patience - and in my case a certain amount of sympathy, as I outlined to him my strictly limited financial resources. That others triumphed where I failed is to their great credit, as also is the large collection of beautifully restored engines, which today grace our rally fields, which at some time during their history lay derelict, watched over and closely guarded by the Edwards family. 'Berkshire Tariff Queen' is just such one of these, which following its purchase from Edwards was restored to a

'BERKSHIRE TARIFF QUEEN'

FOWLER No. 11814 of 1909 at Burbage Wharf c. 1950. *(Photo Road Locomotive Society)*

fine condition, and to date has enjoyed several further owners. Regarding its unusual name, several theories have been advanced for this. The one I prefer, which assumes some credence, is that expounded by Robert Whitehead - the highly respected and acclaimed author on all matters steam - who, in writing to the National Traction Engine Trust's magazine 'Steaming' in the Spring of 1986 concluded, that in the year of its delivery (1909), an extensive campaign was mounted against the importation of European hops, which were eroding the business of UK growers. "In those days.. he continues - hop farms extended into Hampshire and Berkshire. The method of import regulation proposed was by the introduction of tariffs". I presume that the engine's first owner - Mr Stephens - was thus making a statement!

Returning to the Wharf - the engines now dispersed, contracting ceased, the family business assumed the role outlined in the preceding chapter, namely a small farming enterprise carried on by Jack. He continued as such, living with his sister Molly in the farmhouse in which he was born until his death on June 6th, 1991, two days before his eighty-sixth birthday.

That autumn Molly handed in the tenancy of 'The Wharf', returning the key of that lovely old house to the estate office, which brought to an end the 'Falls' occupation of that chosen spot after a period of one hundred and seventeen years; more than a century in which that family, had lived, loved, grown up and died there - three generations of them. They had farmed, been wharfingers, steam threshing and ploughing contractors through momentous times; times of war and peace - times of severe restriction and limited plenty. They had conducted their affairs and family life in such a way that they had gained the respect and friendship of all with whom they had come in contact, and become so much a facet of everyday life, that they were synonymous with that place. Sadly, then, I recall being told by Molly, that when she finally handed in the key and her tenancy, she received no letter of thanks or expression of any gratitude from the estate! All so different from the day when, in a previous century, the family had arrived at 'the Wharf', under the patronage of George Frederick the second Marquess of Ailesbury - who held his new tenant John Fall in such high esteem that he stated "so long as there is a Fall about, he shall live at the Wharf". How times change!

CHAPTER XII

Whilst undertaking research for and setting down this work, I have become forcibly aware of several facets of business life of days gone by, which reflect particularly well on those involved.

Firstly, I refer in turn to John Fall, the firm's founder then in due time to his son George, both of whom for many years shouldered the burden as head of the family. Families whose every comfort and security depended upon their sense of duty, their judgment, their considerable business acumen and their own daily toil. I marvel at their resourcefulness and their ability to not only work physically, but at the same time undertake a vast array of demanding regimes. Each in his own turn not only had to organise his farming enterprise, the cropping, the stocking, the milk and coal rounds - but to carry out his duties as wharfinger, besides which maintain and secure sufficient work for his steam contracting enterprise, as well as keep account of all financial details. That they were able to do this, in an age when the pony and trap was the predominant form of transport with which to visit their tackle and clients - to search out work to be undertaken and to oft-times collect their recompense, must have entailed herculean feats of endurance. Besides which, without the aid of a secretary or today's modern office equipment, it befell them to keep their own accounts, settle all their bills, render their own accounts, pay their labour and write their own letters. That they surely did this is evidenced by a number of quill-written letters that I have been privileged to see, as well as their Labour and Acreage Book about which I have already written. I stand in awe of their example left for posterity - for they still found time for family life - to play their role as head of the family. The oft-repeated epithet of "Fag Packet Farmer" did surely not apply to these hard worked men.

Folded within the papers of the much-quoted ledger that has survived, the larger of the two, the Acreage and Labour Book, are several scraps of paper and a few letters. These letters open for me a window onto times past, and once more reveal and reinforce that about which we have heard much of days gone by - and which today is sadly lacking in many spheres of life; namely integrity. In the days of which I write, when 'the Falls' went about their steam contracting business, a man's word was his bond, a slap or shake of the hand sufficient to seal any deal, without the need of copious forms of reference and security which befalls modern society. Thus we find these above-mentioned letters, though short in length - and to the point - refreshingly honest in content. Two of which clearly illustrate the 'two-way' nature of this finest of human attributes between farmer and contractor and vice-versa. One dated 16th January 1894 enclosed a cheque for ten guineas to cover some cultivating that had been done twice. It goes on to say that

Hardenhuish Court
Chippenham
Jan 16th 1894

Dear Sir

I understood
by Mr Ferris that your
charge for cultivating
was 11/- per acre for
doing it twice, I
have enclosed cheque
for ten guineas, with
which I hope you

will be satisfied
as it was so late
in the season I am afraid
it has done but
very little good the
rain coming directly
upon it, your bill
was mislaid or I
should have sent it
before

Yours very truly
F. H.

One of the letters
referred to on the
opposite page.

71

he (the farmer) trusted Mr Fall would be satisfied with the cheque as "it was so late in the season - I'm afraid it has done very little good the rain coming directly upon it".

Another one dated January 4th 1896, informs Mr Fall that:-

"My piece of land is 20 acres - with hedges and half the Green Lane, and some of it is down with grass as near as I can say your Steamers done 17_ acres - your men will know near what it is".

Yours truly

Underneath which in pencil Mr Fall had written 8 acres twice!

Nevertheless, how refreshing these letters are, as in each case they reveal the goodwill that existed one with another, which had undoubtedly been accumulated as year followed year - a true countryman's code.

In Chapter VII I made brief mention of hearing my first hand accounts from some who either recalled the visit of 'the Falls' steamers to their village or farm where they themselves worked or who in some cases received employment from this family. In the first category I mention Doug Smith - a man whose retirement has been enlivened by his many appearances at local steam engine rallies, either as an exhibitor aboard his Burrell traction engine No. 3068 of 1909 or else by entertaining the spectators as commentator. His home was in the Wiltshire village of East Grafton, where his father traded as village baker for a period of forty-six years. Nearby his home, adjacent to the bakery was a small village pond, where passing enginemen replenished the tenders of their mighty steeds. Doug recalls receiving his first ride on an engine in just such circumstances - "Jack Fall lifted me up off my trike and placed me on the coal in the tender and gave me a ride for a short distance as he moved off".

The late Jack Holloway was a remarkable man who, in his retirement, organised a series of steam engine rallies in his home village of Seend, near Melksham in Wiltshire - which raised over £26,000 with which a famed Memorial Pavilion in the village was re-built. During the latter part of his retirement however, he took up his pen and, rejoicing in the pseudonym of "Fowler Jack", he wrote copious letters to the National Preservation Press as well as a potted version of "My Life Story in Steam". Through this he gradually revealed facets of his remarkable life and the harshness of his early days. His mother died at an early age and with his father "taking to drink" - his grandmother being unable to cope, he was sent to the Pewsey Workhouse there he stayed until aged ten, when his father regained employment and taking on a housekeeper - he was allowed home. Jack later became a soldier with the Wiltshire regiment, being evacuated from Dunkirk - also seeing action in India, the Middle East, Palestine, then via Italy to Germany where he finished his war. Demobilisation for him was followed by sixteen years in the boiler shop of Southern Railways at Ashford, before his return to his native Wiltshire where he became chief welder at an agricultural machinery works until his retirement at the end of 1981.

Through his writings he revealed many details of the Falls establishment at Burbage Wharf - of his father's employ with them as waggoner - "delivering coal around the area: they were coal merchants of repute". He told of playing truant from school to see and be with the engines; of beatings for his wrong-doings, and later as a young man of working both with the threshing and steam ploughing gangs. Within his writing, he reveals much of the role played by the Falls, and those whom they employed in that rural community. Also written 'between the lines' one can easily comprehend the great admiration that he possessed for that family who fulfilled his every childhood fantasy, and who later gave him much needed employment in his early youth. They were indeed 'Masters of their craft'. I deem myself fortunate indeed to have known "Fowler Jack" - to whom I and many others owe a debt of gratitude for setting down for posterity, from first hand knowledge, the everyday life of steam contracting. May he sleep long and rest in peace.

Len Griffiths and Wallace (Wally) Dennis are two highly respected and much loved members of Hungerford community. Now both well retired, my family and I are delighted to number them amongst our closest and dearest friends. As a young boy, Wally Dennis went to Canada, straight after leaving school aged fifteen years, under the "Empire Mission for Boys", a religious mission for which he was recruited by the Rev. Weight, the vicar of his home village Shalbourne. He eagerly went as so many other young boys of large families did also, as, following the end of the Great War, there was but little employment for them at home. He went to work on a farm in the North West Frontier - a barren wilderness of unimaginable vastness, where the main arable crop was a sixty-day stunted variety of wheat. The season of planting to harvest being governed by the harshness of the winters which endured for eight months of the year. He vividly recalls one Christmas day that was so cold, that the mercury did not leave the bulb at the base of the glass.

After eight years spent working on the farm and logging in the forests in wintertime, he returned home where the prospect of employment had not significantly increased, it still being 'between the wars'. Whilst living with his mother at Church Street, Great Bedwyn, there came a knock at the door one day - Billy Dines a ploughman with the local steam ploughing contractors, Fall Bros wanted a plough-hand, "Could he help?" Thus at twenty-four years of age he became a Steam Plough 'Boy' - in the winter of 1937/38. He was in fact to ride the cultivator whilst they broke up two fields of sainfoin, one of 18 acres the other of 24 acres. Those fields had been down to this ley for some fifteen years and had been 'fed-off' by winter grazing of sheep. Wally recalls that the fields, the larger one of which was long and narrow, ran up under the range of chalk hills that closed off the eastern end of the Vale of Pewsey at a place known as 'Starveall Farm'. To

FOWLER BB1 of 1919 at Burbage Wharf. JACK FALL on the left.

74

cultivate the larger field lengthways, the engines had to split it in two, making a false headland in the middle. He states that Jack Fall drove one engine - the right hand one, 'Tricky' Povey drove the other. The fields were cultivated over twice, "the first time over it was'nt too bad, but going over crossways against the ridges! Well, I can remember it now - it was awful"! Incidentally, following these cultivations, the fields were left fallow and 'couched' in time honoured fashioned; it being raked up into clumps and burnt during the next season. Following this work, the engines returned to Burbage Wharf, Wally then having a day or two threshing with the family.

Len Griffiths was born, like both his father and mother before him, in the tiny village of Wilton, which lies to the east of Burbage. A true 'Wiltshire lad', the third child and only son of four children, to Harry and Isabella. His first job on leaving the village school was working for Fred Edwards of Manor Farm. Here he was employed as a junior carter, helping to look after the six heavy draught horses resident on that farm.

Len recalls drawing water to Falls ploughing engines when they visited the farm on a regular basis. Heavy, tiring work, which entailed hand pumping the water from the village pond into the contractor's large, high-wheeled water-cart, then leading the pair of horses - in traces - to wherever the engines happened to be engaged. Work that Len says was "ceaseless, starting early, and going on all day long - as soon as you had filled them up, then they were ready for some more"! This the more especially so, if the field being tilled was some distance from the village centre - the water source. The soil lies heavy in that area, in the fields that sit below the rising chalk downs, and he well remembers watering the engines whilst they were at work in a field which ran uphill - up towards the knoll on which the famed Wilton Windmill stands. A windmill - a notable landmark - which was constructed in 1821 out of fear that the newly opened Kennet and Avon Canal would so severely deplete the waters of the river Kennet and its tributaries that insufficient water would remain with which to operate the many mills in the locality. A fear that was largely unfounded, even though, from its inception until the present day, a constant supply of water throughout the length of the canal has so far eluded it. He tells that on that occasion it was not unduly difficult to 'water-up' the engine that lay along the bottom headland - adjacent to the roadway even though that headland was thick with cloying mud, which stuck to the horses hooves, the water-cart wheels, and his own boots - long before the era of waterproof wellingtons! But to reach the other engine lying under the hedgerow along the top of the field, nearby the windmill - "Well the horses just couldn't manage it". With a resourcefulness that typified that calling, they merely attached a short length of chain between the water-cart and the plough - so that, as the engine pulled the plough uphill towards itself, so too did it assist the horses, which walked steadily beside the plough, no doubt relieved that their burden had been eased. Len recalled walking beside the leading horse,

A fine study of concentration as HARRY FALL steers the plough towards the BB1 Fowler ploughing engine driven by brother BILL FALL at a ploughing demonstration near Winchester (c. 1970) – both engines and plough used that day then owned by T. T. Boughton and Sons Ltd.

(Photo courtesy Cecil Brown)

which did not appear unduly unnerved by the plough, presumably used to the cleaving sound of the earth being turned.

These then I am sure, are but few of the recollections that must remain within the memories of many of the senior citizens of this locality concerning the Fall family. Others there must be who could also recall either having worked with them or having witnessed their comings and goings at first hand. Nevertheless, I deem it essential that the part played by that family of agriculturalists is recorded for posterity as, before many more years have passed, there will be but few remaining who will be able to tell, by personal experience, their exploits.

Whilst I have recorded that the family's enterprise has comprised not only farming, retail coal and milk rounds, but also having been wharfingers; undoubtedly the part for which they have received most recognition and lasting fame, must perforce be their role as steam threshing and ploughing contractors. I believe this to be justified as their tenure of the Wharf Farm, in total almost one hundred and twenty years, had indeed spanned the whole era of commercial, agricultural contracting in which harnessed steam was its power source. They had been in at the beginning - the early 1870's and plied their trade up and down their chosen Vale of Pewsey and immediate locality, during a parlous time for agriculture. At times one of depression, then restrictions through two World Wars, which brought with them not only shortages of labour and raw materials - when the countryman's innate ability to make do and mend manifested itself to great advantage, but which curiously provided much employment for their services with a corresponding increase in the family's prosperity. Times there were also of great change and uncertainty, mirrored in the rural economy by the period between the wars. Yes, they had been through it all - and continued for more than a century to play their part well in the lives of that community. Their livelihood and that of their farming neighbours depended upon their ability to prosper and by so doing being able to offer an invaluable service to those they visited on an annual basis to thresh their corn and till their land. Little wonder then that today, wherever and whenever older countrymen gather in these parts to talk of times past, be it in the warmth of the snug of some village hostelry or the open acres of some steam engine rally field, when the topic turns to steam engines - inevitably, with an air of affection and admiration, they will mention the "Falls of Burbage Wharf".

BILL FALL driving Aveling and Porter roller No. 10762 of 1923 Registration MF4008 on the left. HARRY FALL driving Burrell roller No. 3991 of 1924 Registration AF9803 on the right – at an Appleford Rally in the late 1960's. *(Photo courtesy Cecil Brown)*

BIBLIOGRAPHY

THE WARDENS OF SAVERNAKE FOREST - CEDRIC THE MARQUESS OF AILESBURY - PUBLISHED BY ROUTLEDGE & KEGAN PAUL 1949

THE HISTORY OF SAVERNAKE FOREST - PUBLISHED BY ROUTLEDGE & KEGAN PAUL 1962

BRUNEL AND AFTER - BY ARCHIBALD WILLIAMS - PUBLISHED BY WALWIN 1976

MIDLAND & SOUTH WESTERN JUNCTION RLY VOL 1 BY DAVID BARTHOLOMEW -PUBLISHED BY WILD SWAN PUBLICATIONS LIMITED

SYLVAN SAVERNAKE AND ITS STORY - BY W MAURICE ADAMS - PUBLISHED BY ADAMS C.1910

PROGRESS IN ENGLISH FARMING SYSTEMS - BY C. S. ORWIN - PUBLISHED BY OXFORD CLARENDON PRESS 1930

STEAM IS THE ESSENCE - BY R. A. WHITEHEAD - PUBLISHED BY R. A. WHITEHEAD & PARTNERS 1993

'THE ENBORNE QUEEN'

AVELING & PORTER   6 hp 10 ton, single cylinder, owned by C. J. BROWN. DRIVER: BILL FALL.
c. early 1970's.